*Ed Glin*

# 111 Places in Yorkshire That You Shouldn't Miss

*Photographs by David Taylor*

emons:

For Lindsay Sutton, 'Mr Yorkshire'

© Emons Verlag GmbH
© Photographs by David Taylor, except:
Doncaster's Winning Post (ch. 18): Shutterstock/Mick Atkins
Pontefract Hermitage (ch. 58, top image): picture alliance/empics | John Giles
Pontefract Hermitage (ch. 58, bottom image): mauritius images/
Paul Heaton/Alamy
Canal Lock from Hell (ch. 86): mauritius images/AlanWrigley/Alamy
York's Terrible Tower (ch. 104): pixabay.com/PublicDomainPictures/17902
© Cover icon: private
Layout: Eva Kraskes, based on a design
by Lübbeke | Naumann | Thoben
Maps: altancicek.design, www.altancicek.de
Basic cartographical information from Openstreetmap,
© OpenStreetMap-Mitwirkende, OdbL
Editing: Rosalind Horton
Printing and binding: Grafisches Centrum Cuno, Calbe
Printed in Germany 2022
ISBN 978-3-7408-1167-9
Second edition, November 2022

*Guidebooks for Locals & Experienced Travellers*
Join us in uncovering new places around the world at
www.111places.com

# Foreword

This is a big, big book. Some 111 Places volumes cover a small locale: London's East End or one city, Liverpool. This 111 covers England's biggest county, and the county keeps getting bigger. This is because proud parochialists have come to remember that Middlesbrough shouldn't be in the strange anomaly Cleveland, or Hull in the hopelessly contrived Humberside, but should go back where they belong, to Yorkshire. To go back to how it was before Ted Heath needlessly messed up the boundaries, chopped up a few bits into a Greater Manchester dog's dinner, and reconstituted the much-loved East, West and North Ridings into the West, North and South Yorkshires.

This book honours proper Yorkshire – the Tees as the northern border, a choppy sea of foam and fresh fish on the east, the Humber, the Went and some fiddly bits on the south, and something called Lancashire on the west. Inside is everywhere you'd expect at first thought, from Barnsley, Beverley and Bradford to York and the Yorkshire Dales, and then many you would never think of, like Liversedge, Malton and Marsden. Leeds, Sheffield and York are not covered in detail as there are separate volumes dealing with those cities alone.

In limiting the number of entries to the necessary 111 in a place as huge as Yorkshire, some locations have had to remain in the sub shack. I've tried to avoid the clichéd and hackneyed, so there's no Nora Batty, *Heartbeat* Country and *Emmerdale*, farm or not. Far more important in a book like this are the Leeds Refectory, where The Who recorded *Live at Leeds*; Ann Lister's Shibden Hall; Bettys Tea Rooms (no apostrophe); the spookily abandoned church of Heptonstall; twisting *Temenos* by the Tees; Batley Variety Club, which Dean Martin turned down; the canal lock from hell in Sowerby Bridge; Ted Hughes' Kingdom of Elmet; the peculiar of Masham; and to honour Yorkshire's greatest modern-day cultural phenomenon, Cabaret Voltaire ('Always work, go to church, do right. Respect those in authority').

*Ed Glinert*

# 111 Places

# 1__ The Aiggin Stone
*Welcome to Yorkshire!*

This ancient stone, scratched with a Latin cross and the mysterious letters 'I.T.', heralds the ancient entry to Yorkshire from Lancashire. It also marks the boundary between the rolling gentle hills of the South and the rugged landscapes of the North.

Although some believe the Aiggin Stone to be Roman in origin, it first appeared on a map, an engineer's map, in 1800. It may have been a milestone or simply a marker to guide people on their way during fog. The architect Herbert Collins writing in 1950 assumed the word 'Aiggin' to be a corruption of Agger, Latin for a pile or mound, or from the French aiguille, a needle. In 1965, James Maxim described the stone as 'an irregular block of gritstone seven feet long, tapering from two feet six inches to two feet wide, about ten inches thick. On one face is an incised cross with the ends of the arms slightly expanded'.

The stone mysteriously disappeared in the 20th century. It was found some time after laid in moorland heather and put back to its rightful spot in 1933. Since then it's been knocked over a few times, but it's now back where it should be. It used to be seven foot but has shrunk due to being pushed over and attacked.

Finding the stone is not easy. Look for the White House pub on the A58 Ripponden to Halifax road, itself a mid-18th-century packhorse route near the Pennine Way and Blackstone Edge reservoir. From the pub, cross the road and walk along the track below the disused quarry till you meet a straight uphill path. The stone is at the top. From there it is possible on a clear day to see Manchester city centre's new skyscrapers and the mountains of north Wales.

There's just one problem. Due to nonsensical 1974 boundary changes, the Aiggin Stone currently resides in a reformatted Lancashire. Elsewhere the boundary between the two counties is often vague and has led to hundreds of years of disputes.

**Address** One mile south of the A 58 and Blackstone Edge Reservoir, three miles east of Littleborough | **Getting there** Train to Littleborough station | **Hours** Accessible 24 hours | **Tip** Fancy meeting another historic rock? Robin Hood's Bed overlooks the very edge of the ridge. Head over the stile by the fence opposite and trek a half-mile south to where the legendary hero enjoyed a well-deserved nap, protected by some of his followers.

# 2 Barnsley Main Colliery

*Coal not dole*

It's a sight that used to be ubiquitous across South Yorkshire: the winding gear of a colliery. But since a change in government policy in the 1980s over how energy should be supplied, the nation's coal mines have disappeared, one by one, which makes the survival of the Barnsley Main Colliery winding engine house and pit head structures, dating back to 1900, all the more rewarding.

To the mining community of Yorkshire the remains of Barnsley Main have a special and sad connection. It is the last surviving structure associated with the 1866 Oaks Colliery Disaster, England's worst mining accident. On 12 December, 1866, 361 miners and rescuers died at the colliery following a series of methane gas explosions. Barnsley Main's No. 2 shaft was deepened further in 1916, to reach a new seam, the Fenton, using machine-cutting for the first time, and was connected to the Oaks with expansion in the 1930s.

After World War II, nationalisation saw the mine pass to the National Coal Board. Yet on 7 May, 1947 there was another disaster. Twenty-two men were killed. One died from a fractured skull while others died from the effects of breathing in methane gas. The colliery closed in 1991, after which the buildings were cleared and the site landscaped. All openings were bricked up to prevent unauthorised entry; however, the headstocks and winding engine house of No. 2 shaft were retained.

The vast South Yorkshire coalfield lies at the foot of the Pennines, and Barnsley's was always the main section. Coal had been mined from shallow seams since mediaeval times. The coal is still there but closure followed in the 1980s when Margaret Thatcher's government launched a political attack on the power of the National Union of Mineworkers, which is still based in the town. When Arthur Scargill became president in 1981 it had around 170,000 members. It is now down to double figures.

**Address** 55 Oaks Lane, Barnsley, S70 3ET | **Getting there** Off the A 628, two miles east of Barnsley station; bus 32, 198, 22x, 222 or 226 from Barnsley Interchange station | **Hours** Accessible 24 hours | **Tip** Head south down the M1 to south Rotherham and High Field Lane, the site of one of the most appalling miscarriages of justice in British history – Orgreave. On 18 June, 1984, during the lengthy miners' strike, some of the worst industrial violence ever witnessed ensued as pickets clashed with police.

# 3_ Dickie Bird Statue

*Beyond the boundary*

West of the Pennines, it's football; east of the Pennines, or on them: cricket. It's unusual for sports officials to become as famous as the players, but it was different with legendary umpire Harold 'Dickie' Bird.

Barnsley-born Bird played first-class cricket for Yorkshire and Leicestershire but managed only two centuries in 93 appearances before his career was cut short by a knee injury. He then took up the impossible job of umpiring, which he performed in a remarkable 66 Test Matches as well as three World Cup Finals. The affection with which the public long held Bird, saw him sell more than a million copies of his autobiography. His many eccentricities have added to his loveable image. Drama always seemed to be happening to him. At a 1973 Test against the West Indies his fellow umpire, Arthur Fagg, refused to continue in protest against the conduct of the West Indian players. When play was interrupted at Lord's by an IRA bomb scare, Bird and the players sat down in the centre of the pitch, knowing it was safer than being in the stands. The best story was when he was on a bus near The Oval in south London. He noticed the conductor was wearing a rather fetching white hat similar to the ones he usually sported. He asked the conductor where he obtained it from: 'Man, haven't you heard of Mr Dickie Bird? This is one of his hats. I took it off his head at the World Cup final … we all ran onto the field and I won the race.'

In 2009, this life-sized bronze statue by Graham Ibbeson was erected in his hometown. It shows him standing in a familiar pose: one arm outstretched and pointing to show that a batsman is out. Over the next four years, rowdy revellers left bras, panties and condoms hanging from his outstretched finger, until the statue was raised onto a five-foot high plinth, which only encourages pranksters to try harder now to catch Bird out.

**Address** Church Lane, Barnsley, S70 2DP | **Getting there** The statue is off the A635, just north of St Mary's Church; train to Barnsley Interchange or Barnsley station and a 12-minute walk; bus 93, 95 or 95a | **Hours** Accessible 24 hours | **Tip** A mile or so south in Locke Park is a statue of Joseph Locke. Fans of the mid-20th- century Irish tenor of the same name, the so-called 'Singing Bobby', might be disappointed to discover this Joseph Locke is the early 19th-century railway engineer who was an apprentice to George Stephenson. So you won't hear this Joseph Locke's song.

# 4_ Batley Variety Club
*Variety is the spice of live*

No tour of England by a comedian, middle-of-the-road singer or cabaret act in the 1960s and 1970s would be complete without a stint at the legendary Batley Variety Club. At its peak, during the heyday of what the BBC used to call light entertainment, the club had 300,000 members, who might expect to see Tom Jones one week, Morecambe and Wise or maybe Ken Dodd the next – Rod Hull and Emu if they were unlucky.

The club was built in 1967 by James and Betty Corrigan on an old sewage site. When the local authority discovered the building had been constructed too close to the road it had to be started again from scratch. It was rebuilt with a low ceiling that aided intimacy and could hold as many as 1,750 punters. The food was served in obligatory baskets – no rubber chickens, apparently – aided by plastic cutlery so that the acts wouldn't be disturbed by the sound of clinking.

The Corrigans had done their research in Las Vegas, but the headline act on the opening night, 27 March, 1967, was not Frank Sinatra or, best of all, Johnny Mathis, but the terminally naff Irish vocal group the Bachelors. Would the venture work? Even the PR lady noted that 'most people in Batley were mill workers in greasy overalls, inhaling smoke from the chimneys'. Nevertheless, Louis Armstrong and Roy Orbison came, although Dean Martin's people knocked back the £45,000 offer, politely explaining that their man wouldn't leave his bed for a Geoff Hurst for such a piddly amount, or words to that effect. Shirley Bassey did however say 'yes' to an invitation for dinner, and donned her fur coat, heels and t'ing, expecting a trip in a Rolls-Royce to a posh restaurant, only to discover the menu was fish and chips in the back of the van.

Batley Variety club closed in 1978, soon reopening as the tastelessly named Crumpets night club. Now it's a gym. No, Olga Korbut isn't the star act.

**Address** Bradford Road, Batley, WF17 6JD, +44 (0)1924 442122 | **Getting there** Just south of Batley station, off the B 6124; bus 183, 281 or 624A | **Tip** Batley Central Club at No. 436 is a proper old-fashioned Yorkshire working men's club with concerts every Saturday night, jazz on a Sunday afternoon but no real ale.

# 5 _ Beverley Market Cross
*Don't make the market cross*

They used to stand in the middle of every town – the official middle, no less – but nowadays finding an authentic market cross is like finding a high-street blacksmith when your horse loses his shoe. Yet in Beverley, eight miles north of Hull, the cross still proudly stands.

Market crosses marked out the market area and were where important declarations, such as the death of a monarch and their replacement, would be made. Nowadays they're likely to be used only when festooned with Christmas decorations. Beverley's was designed by Theophilus Shelton in 1714. It consists of pairs of coupled Romanesque Doric columns and displays the coats of arms of the MPs of the time, those of Beverley and of Queen Anne, then on the throne.

Beverley, which means beaver stream, was founded around A.D. 700 by a mysterious bishop who became known as St John of Beverley. It was a place of pilgrimage in the Middle Ages, when one of the country's greatest churches, Beverley Minster, was built. It was also a leading centre for brick making, which caused such foul smells that a by-law was passed in 1461 that stated 'on account of fouling of the air and destruction of fruit trees no-one is to make a kiln nearer than the kilns that are already built'.

Because Beverley escaped the harshness of the Industrial Revolution it has remained one of the most sought-after locations in the area, described by the legendary architectural historian Nikolaus Pevsner as 'among the finest of England's small country towns'. In 2014, a bizarre ceremony held at the Cross saw the commemoration of the 300th anniversary of the accession of George I, a German who should never have been crowned given he was 50th in line when appointed. This was followed by the reading of the Riot Act, a repressive measure created to stifle legitimate protest, and a volley of muskets fired by a band of soldiers in period dress.

**Address** Lairgate, Beverley, HU17 8EE | **Getting there** The cross is on the A164 in the centre of town, natch. It is a seven-minute walk from Beverley bus station. | **Hours** Accessible 24 hours | **Tip** On Friars Lane, a short stroll from the Minster, is a much-restored 600-year-old Dominican Friary, mentioned by Geoffrey Chaucer in *The Canterbury Tales*, now a youth hostel.

# 6_ Beverley Sanctuary Stone
*Give me sanctuary!*

It's not just a strange lump of stone with a bizarre guard around it. It's all that remains of a rare mediaeval sanctuary cross signifying that criminals – even murderers – could seek pardon for their misdemeanours here.

In most cases sanctuary was a church. Fugitives would enter the churchyard but often fail to make it to the church itself, having been caught by a pursuer. This would rise to £140 if the criminal had reached the choir. An apprehender taking down a felon at the altar might forfeit his own life. Once criminals had gained sanctuary they were allowed to stay for 30 days to seek pardon. If this failed, they were escorted out of the sanctuary area.

In Beverley, the sanctuary applied to the whole town. This remarkable arrangement was granted by King Athelstan, the first Saxon king of England, when St John of Beverley won the Battle of Brunanburh in AD 937, a battle that preserved the unity of the whole of England. William the Conqueror then later sent a ruthless warrior, Toustain, to desecrate Beverley Minster and drag out those who had taken refuge there. But when Toustain approached the altar St John felled him with a blinding light that swelled his limbs and sent his head revolving in a full circle, *Exorcist* style.

Beverley's sanctuary was known as the Peace of St John and extended for a league (a mile and a half) from the Minster, where St John of Beverley is buried. The outer limits were marked with stone crosses like this, but this stone was lucky to survive. Many were destroyed after the Reformation of the 16th century, and then again by iconoclasts during the subsequent Puritan period.

Other Yorkshire sanctuaries include Ripon and York. Although mediaeval sanctuary no longer exists, the idea of sanctuary chimes with contemporary ideas about refugees seeking asylum. The British Library houses the original Beverley Sanctuary Book.

**Address** A 164, Bentley, just south of junction with the A 1079 | **Hours** Accessible 24 hours | **Tip** In Beverley Minster, one of the most majestic churches in the country, there is a Sanctuary Chair, one of only two in existence.

# 7__ The Five Rise Locks

*Lock up your boaters*

This cuddly-close collection of locks on the Leeds–Liverpool Canal is an engineering masterpiece. It dates back to the 1770s when John Longbotham of Halifax, the canal's first engineer, created five locks built like a staircase in which the lower gate forms the upper gate of the next. The dimensions of the locks system are mind-boggling. There is a 60-foot drop over a horizontal distance of 320 feet with a steep gradient of 1 in 5. The gates at the bottom are the tallest lock gates in the British canal system.

Pioneers met at the Sun Inn in Bradford on 2 July, 1766 to discuss building a canal. James Brindley, the country's most knowledgeable canal engineer was hired. His survey identified a route of 109 miles and a cost of £259,777 (around £40 million in today's prices). The first section, from Bingley to Skipton, which ironically was lock-free, opened in 1773. Canal builders across the country were so impressed with the Bingley five-rise system, they wanted their own. In 1805 Leicester came up with a 10-lock staircase at Foxton on the Grand Union Canal.

At the locks' opening in 1774, thousands gathered to watch the first boat make the journey. It did so in a barely believable 28 minutes, which led the *Leeds Intelligencer* newspaper to wax about 'the ringing of church bells, the firing of guns by the neighbouring militia, the shouts of the spectators and the marks of satisfaction so important an event merits'.

As industry became mechanised and more powerful in the late 18th century, the Leeds–Liverpool became a vital trans-Pennine link. Bradford merchants used it to send textiles to the port of Liverpool, while in Lancashire traders wanted cheap coal from Yorkshire. Trade on the canal continued until the 1980s. Now that the industrial purpose has gone, it is best used as the start of a route of 16 miles of lock-free cruising on the canal in the Yorkshire Dales.

**Address** Leeds–Liverpool Canal, east of the A650, Bingley | **Getting there** 200 yards south-east of Crossflatts station | **Hours** Accessible 24 hours | **Tip** As the signpost here proves, it's closer to walk to Leeds than Liverpool at this part of the Leeds–Liverpool Canal. Leeds is 16 miles; Liverpool 111 miles.

# 8___ Dickens' Dotheboys Hall
*Spare the rod…*

It looks so inconspicuous now, but this mundane residential block was William Shaw's Academy, which inspired one of the most infamous and frightening schools in English literature: Dotheboys Hall from Charles Dickens' 1839 novel *Nicholas Nickleby*.

Dotheboys Hall is a brutal North Yorkshire establishment run by Wackford Squeers, the onomatopoeically named headmaster. Squeers is a cruel, one-eyed, money-grabbing sadist who mistreats, starves and beats the boys. The water for bathing is always cold and there are no towels. Dickens claimed Squeers was based not on one individual Yorkshire schoolmaster, but we now know he said such to avoid being sued for libel. In fact, the inspiration for Squeers was William Shaw himself. An infamous court case of the time saw Shaw brought to court by the parents of a boy blinded through neglect. When Dickens arrived at the school for research in February 1838 the headmaster was suspicious and wouldn't let him in.

The advert placed in the novel to entice recruits sums it up perfectly: 'Youth are boarded, clothed, booked, furnished with pocket-money, provided with all necessaries, instructed in all languages living and dead, mathematics, orthography, geometry, astronomy, trigonometry, the use of the globes, algebra, single stick (if required), writing, arithmetic and fortification.' This was based on a real-life notice Shaw released, which explained how 'Youth are carefully instructed in the English, Latin, and Greek languages, writing, common and decimal arithmetic, bookkeeping, mensuration, &c., and are provided with board, clothes, and every necessary, at 20 guineas per annum each. No vacations. N.B. The French language 2 guineas per annum extra.'

After the novel's publication, there was a public outcry that forced many such schools, including this, to close down. The property has since been divided into flats.

**Address** The Street, Bowes, DL12 | **Getting there** The former school is two miles south of Barnard Castle on the A66 | **Hours** Viewable from the outside only | **Tip** At Jock House Barn, a short distance south on the way to the River Greta, you can walk with beautiful beasts at Teesdale Alpacas.

# 9__ Seductive Silver Swan
*Awesome antiquated automaton in amazing abode*

Much visited and admired, this glorious swan is a moving mechanical device or automaton, held in a glass case, that mimics a real-life animalian version. The feature has been placed in a lane of glass rods surrounded by silver leaves, and includes a music box. When the silver swan is wound the music plays, the figure turns its head from side to side, bends down to eat a fish, and the rods rotate making it look like flowing water. The whole spectacle lasts about 30 seconds and takes place every day at 2pm.

The Silver Swan of Bowes dates back to the 18th century. It was shown off at the 1867 World Fair in Paris, where it was spotted by Mark Twain who wrote in *Innocents Abroad* that it had 'a living grace about his movement and a living intelligence in his eyes'. It was bought from a Parisian jeweller five years later. But which is the bigger attraction: the swan or the breathtaking baroque building that houses it?

Bowes is an astonishing sight, an enormous 1870s château-like building, the work of John and Josephine Bowes. John Bowes was an old Etonian, the son of the 10th Earl of Strathmore, who inherited his father's riches but not the title. When he married Parisian actress Joséphine Coffin-Chevallier in 1852 they dreamt of creating a world-class museum. As Joséphine laid the foundation stone in 1869 she announced: 'I am laying the bottom stone and you, Mr Bowes, will lay the top stone.' But John died in 1885 and never did carry out Josephine's wish. The museum opened in June 1892, attracting more than 60,000 visitors in its first year. It contains one of the most spectacular art collections in the North. *A Miracle of the Holy Sacrament* by Sassetta comes from a Sienese altarpiece dating back to 1423–26. *The Harnessing of the Horses of the Sun* by Tiepolo of Venice shows Apollo, the Sun god, about to enter his chariot and journey across the sky.

**Address** The Bowes Museum, Barnard Castle, DL12 8NP, +44 (0)1833 690606, www.thebowesmuseum.org.uk | **Getting there** Just east of the A 67 in the centre of the town; train to Darlington station | **Hours** Daily 10am–5pm | **Tip** Less than a half-mile to the west is Barnard Castle, a pleasant market town with eponymous castle that would have remained in semi-obscurity as far as the rest of Britain was concerned, until Dominic Cummings, the prime minister's special adviser, drove there from Durham 50 miles away to test his eyesight at the height of the 2020 Covid-19 lockdown.

# 10___Billy Liar's Cemetery
### *William, it was really nothing*

If not the greatest ever British film, then, as Brian Clough, the greatest ever Yorkshireman, might have said, *Billy Liar* is certainly in the top one. The 1963 screen version of Keith Waterhouse's comedy classic story of the frustrated undertakers' clerk with the ludicrously solipsistic imagination gives Bradford the full Hollywood treatment. It also boasts of a starlit cast: Tom Courtenay as Billy Fisher, Julie Christie as his never-to-be-consummated love interest, Wilfred Pickles, Rodney Bewes and Leonard Rossiter. Its director, John Schlesinger, later made such classics as *Marathon Man* (1976).

As he dallies with three different girls, and his dreams become ever more surreal and megalomaniacal, Billy longs to escape his humdrum existence and heads to London to become a novelist or maybe a scriptwriter. His attempts to create the great English novel falter on his inability to decide what to call himself as he hovers over the typewriter without a word written. 'Bill Fisher, Billy Fisher, William T. Fisher …'.

Many scenes take place in Bradford, and of all those, Undercliffe Cemetery, where the ridiculous hero cajoles one of his many girlfriends, is the least changed. Fans do the full Bradford Billy Liar tour, also taking in the bland semi on Hinchliffe Avenue, Baildon, where the Fisher family live, and the undertakers where Billy works for the incorrigible Mr Shadrach, superbly named after a character in the Old Testament Book of *Daniel* who escapes the fire, played with appropriate cynicism by Leonard Rossiter.

What makes *Billy Liar* is its northernness; predictably comic book but still hilarious and unforgettable. A highlight is when the crusty undertakers' owner, played by the elderly Finlay Currie (Magwitch in David Lean's *Great Expectations*), chides Billy for calling him 'Mr Duxbury'. 'It's Councillor Duxbury. You wouldn't call Lord Harwood mister. Think on.'

**Address** Undercliffe Cemetery, 127 Undercliffe Lane, Bradford, BD3 0QD,
+44 (0)1274 642276, www.undercliffecemetery.co.uk | **Getting there** The cemetery is in
north-east Bradford, off the A658 near its junction with the A6177; train to Bradford
Interchange station and a 30-minute walk; bus 687 from Bradford interchange station |
**Hours** Daily 7.30am – 9pm | **Tip** Peel Park on the other side of the A658 is a superb
example of a Victorian park, replete with Italianate lodges, classical structures and sculptures
of the great and good.

# 11__Bradford City FC Fire

*Grim reminder of an avoidable tragedy*

By the mid-1980s, football had reached its aesthetic peak as a spectator sport, but conditions for the fans had deteriorated to their worst levels. This was the decade of the Heysel Stadium Disaster on 29 May, 1985 when Juventus fans were killed at the European Cup final in Brussels. Four years later in April 1989 came the Hillsborough Stadium disaster in Sheffield when 96 Liverpool fans were killed during a human crush. But the first of three great tragedies that decade came on Saturday, 11 May, 1985 at a Third Division match between Bradford City, at home to Lincoln City.

During the last game of the season a fire ripped through the main stand at 3.40pm. In only four minutes, aided by the wind, it killed 56 spectators and injured at least 250. Some were trapped in their seats. Others who rushed to the back of the stand found, for reasons that no one will ever understand, that the exit doors were locked, and burned to death there. Commentator John Helm who was working at the ground explained in a newspaper interview how the fire started when 'a man over from Australia for the game tried to extinguish a cigarette on the floor but it slipped through a hole. A minute later he saw a small plume of smoke, so he poured his coffee on it, but a minute later there was suddenly a bigger whoosh of smoke, so they went to get a steward. By the time they got back, the whole thing had taken off'.

The journalist Simon Inglis, who has written much about sports stadiums, had warned the club about the build-up of litter beneath the stand, as had the county council: 'A carelessly discarded cigarette could give rise to a fire risk.' The inquiry into the disaster saw new legislation to improve safety at British football grounds. Every year on 11 May a memorial service takes place here, by German sculptor Joachim Reisner's fascinating structure opposite City Hall. Old-fashioned wooden stands have now disappeared from major football grounds.

**VALLEY PARADE FIRE MEMORIAL**

In memory of the fifty six people who lost their lives
as a result of the fire at this stadium on 11th May 1985

John Douglas Ackroyd (32)
Edmund Anderton (68)
Alexander Shaw Baines (70)
Herbert Bamford (72)
Christopher James Bulmer (11)
Jack Leo Coxon (76)
Leo Anthony Coxon (44)
David James Crabtree (30)
Harry Crabtree (76)
Derek Dempsey (46)
Muriel Firth (65)
Samuel Firth (86)
Andrew Fletcher (11)
Edmund Fletcher (63)
John Fletcher (34)
Peter Fletcher (32)
Nellie Foster (64)
Felix Winspear Greenwood (13)
Peter Greenwood (46)
Rupert Benedict Greenwood (11)
Norman Hall (70)
Peter Halliday (34)
Arthur Hartley (79)
Edith Hindle (79)
Fred Hindle (76)
Moira Helen Hodgson
Eric Hudson (73)
John Hughes (64)

John Hutton (74)
Walter Kerr (76)
Peter Charles Lovell (43)
Jack Ludlam (55)
Gordon McPherson (39)
Irene McPherson (27)
Roy Mason (74)
Frederick Norman Middleton (84)
Harold Mitchell (79)
Elizabeth Muhl (21)
Ernest Normington (75)
Gerald Priestley Ormondroyd (40)
Richard John Ormondroyd (12)
Robert Ian Ormondroyd (12)
Sylvia Lund Pollard (69)
Herbert Price (78)
Amanda Jane Roberts (20)
Jayne Sampson (18)
William Stacey (72)
Craig Albert Stockman (14)
Jayne Ashley Stockman (16)
Trevor John Stockman (38)
Howard Turner (41)
Sarah Turner (16)
Simon Neil Ward (18)
Robert Wedgeworth (72)
William James West (78)
Adrian Mark Wright (11)

**Address** Centenary Square, Bradford, BD1 1HY | **Getting there** West of the A 6181, 400 yards north-west of Bradford Interchange station | **Hours** Accessible 24 hours | **Tip** One of the square's many features is the mirror pool, which contains the highest fountain in any British city, shooting water 100 feet into the air. Alongside are more than 100 smaller fountains.

# 12 City Hall Clock Tower
*The bells, the bells!*

The late 19th century was the era of building great Gothic town halls across the country. This was a particular feature of the new northern cities forged during the Industrial Revolution that now had democratically elected councils for the first time and wanted the grandest of homes to show off the fact.

Fittingly the city, alongside Manchester and Leeds, can boast the grandest, most magnificent, most flamboyant of all the northern town halls. It was designed in the 1870s by Lockwood and Mawson, and on the façade features an array of statues of English monarchs, as well as Oliver Cromwell, the latter often used as a symbol of independence in the North. But the most majestic feature is the bell and clock tower, 200 feet high. It was inspired by the Palazzo Vecchio in Florence and contains 13 bells, first rung at the opening in 1873. They now ring every 15 minutes and play tunes at midday and late afternoon as well as carols in December.

People who have never been to Bradford might have seen the hall in a variety of well-known films, in particular the kitchen sink classic *Room at the Top,* starring Laurence Harvey and the Oscar-winning Simone Signoret. Tours take in the Victorian prison cells used in a number of TV shows including *Peaky Blinders* and from which the legendary escape artist Harry Houdini managed to break free in as long a time as 20 minutes during a publicity stunt in 1904.

For millions of *Daily Telegraph* readers, at the end of the 20th century Bradford's municipal status was hilariously mocked in the long-running Peter Simple column starring the fictitious Bradford alderman Jabez Foodbotham – 'the 25-stone, iron-watch-chained, crag-visaged, grim-booted Lord Mayor of Bradford and perpetual chairman of the city's Tramways and Fine Arts Committee', forever poised to reappear from his grave and rescue Bradford from its travails.

Address Norfolk Gardens, Bradford, BD1 1UH | Getting there A 6181, 200 yards north-west of Bradford Interchange station | Hours Normal working hours | Tip A truncheon's throw from City Hall on Centenary Square is the Bradford Police Museum, which concentrates on policing styles and strategies from the days of a clip round the ear and 'I'll be having a word with your father, sonny.'

# 13___Delius

*'To be sung of a summer night on the water'*

England doesn't have many successful classical composers, yet here's a major figure hailing from Bradford: Frederick Theodore Albert Delius (1862–1934), commemorated with Amber Hiscott's majestic sculpture.

Delius' real first name was Fritz. He was born to German émigré parents who came to Bradford to work in the wool trade that made the city so important. Delius' father, Julius, sent the young Fritz to Florida to manage an orange plantation. There he fathered a child with a local black woman, something so shocking for the time he had to leave. He went to study composition in Leipzig, Germany, and there met fellow composers Grieg, Ravel, and the artists Edvard Munch and Paul Gaugin, before settling in Paris. The conductor and impresario Thomas Beecham promoted Delius back in Britain and secured regular performances of his work, although nowadays it's his contemporary, Edward Elgar, who gets all the plaudits.

When Delius became wheelchair bound in his latter years, a young English admirer, Eric Fenby, volunteered to be an unpaid amanuensis. This saw Delius adding a codicil to his will so that future royalties would be used to support an annual concert of works by young composers. Delius died at his French home in June 1934. He wanted to be buried in his own garden but the French authorities forbade it and so he's at rest in Surrey.

Many Delius compositions evoke nature – *Appalachia*, *Sea Drift* and his best-known work, *On Hearing the First Cuckoo in Spring*. He has also been well-served by other cultural figures, such as Kate Bush with her 1980 song 'Delius (Song of Summer)'. In Ken Russell's BBC TV film *Song of Summer*, a wheelchair-bound Delius is talking in his front garden to fellow composer Percy Grainger when the latter suddenly throws a cricket ball over the house and races through the house with the wheelchair to catch the ball in the back garden.

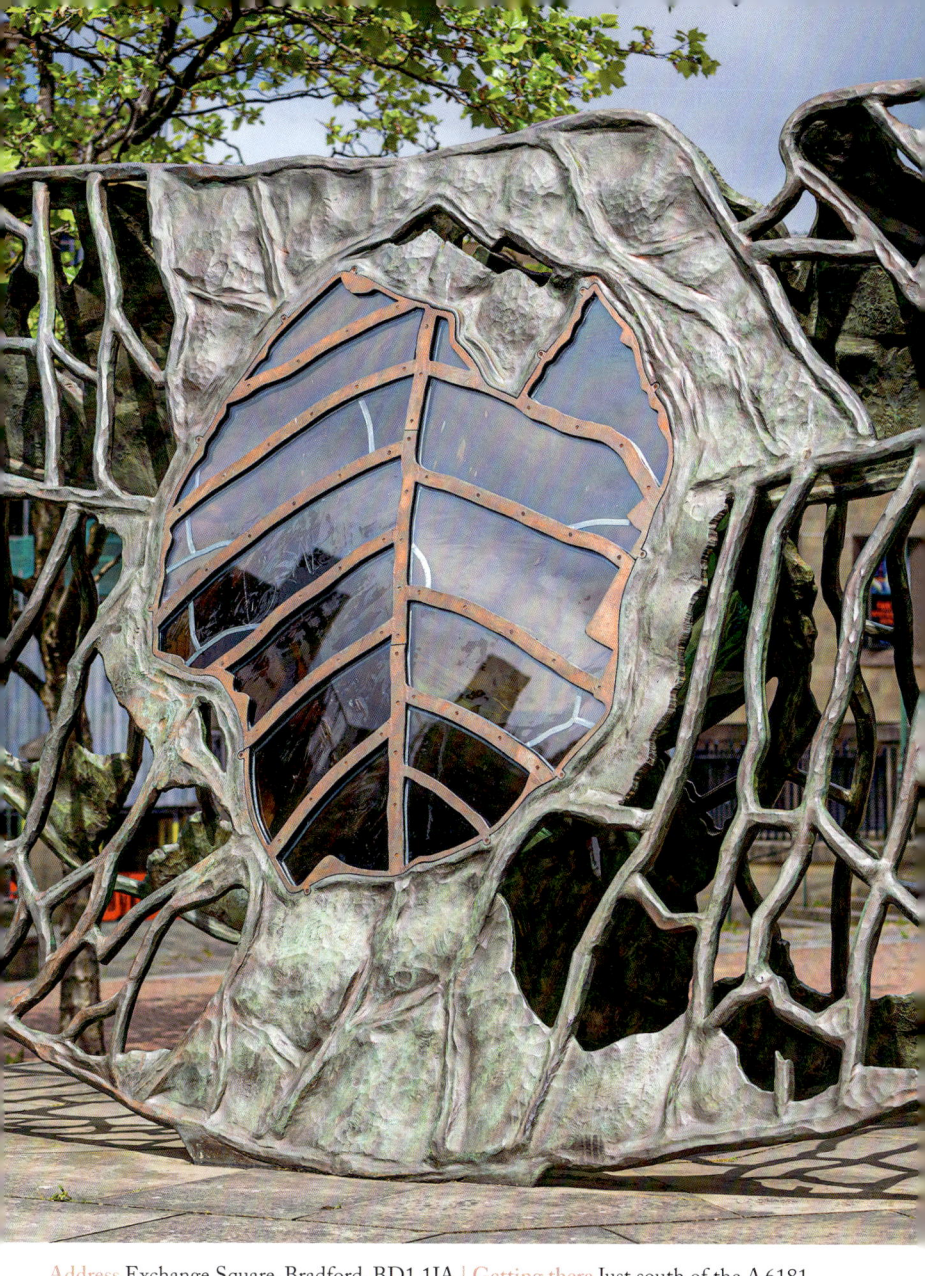

**Address** Exchange Square, Bradford, BD1 1JA | **Getting there** Just south of the A6181, 300 yards north of Bradford Interchange station | **Hours** Accessible 24 hours | **Tip** There are a number of Delius sites in the city, although sadly the Delius Lived Nextdoor pub, surprisingly next door to where Delius lived has been turned into student flats. On East Parade in the Little Germany area, a plaque marks the former offices of 'D. Delius', the composer's father, a German wool merchant. The striking German church on Great Horton Road where Delius' parents were members sports a stained-glass window with the Delius name.

# 14  Museum of the Ever-Changing Name

*It's all the media's fault*

Here's a rare Yorkshire story for what is now called 'the Mainstream Media'. There used to be a fantastic museum in Bradford. It opened in 1983 as the National Museum of Photography, Film & Television and featured Britain's largest cinema screen: the five-storey IMAX screen with six-channel sound. Quadrophonic, too, they said, for those with four ears.

The inhabitants of the beleaguered and increasingly run-down city of Bradford took great pride in its existence. In December 2006 it was renamed the National Media Museum, thereby confusing thousands of potential visitors, although at least it did now feature some of the original apparatus of John Logie Baird, inventor of the television, and the world's first gallery dedicated to exploring the impact of the internet, or what in Bradford is known as th'internet.

In 2013 the managers down in London revealed that cutbacks could force them to close one of the three northern venues run by the capital's Science Museum – and it was Bradford that was going to get it. There was a huge public outcry. The local paper amassed more than 45,000 signatures in opposition, and support came from Martin Scorsese, Monty Python stars and local lad David Hockney.

Predictably it was then announced that the museum's future was saved – as long it changed its name, this time to the National Science and Media Museum, just to remind everyone that London's Science Museum was in charge. To add insult to injury the Royal Photographic Society moved its collection of 400,000 images down south to create an 'international photography resource centre' in London in what one Bradford politician described as 'an appalling act of cultural vandalism'.

Locals have now dubbed the venue 'the National Museum of whatever it's called today'.

**Address** Pictureville, Bradford, BD1 1NQ, +44 (0)330 0580058, www.scienceandmediamuseum.org.uk | **Getting there** Take the A6181 to the centre of town; just west of Bradford Interchange station; bus 571, 576, 640 or 641. The museum is near all the big attractions. | **Hours** Wed–Sun 10am–4pm | **Tip** Bradford's Industrial Museum, north-east of the city centre (235 Moorside Road, BD2 3HP), showcases much earlier forms of technology with permanent displays of textile machinery, steam power, engineering machinery and motor vehicles.

# 15__ Old Labour is born
*Labour was working*

This people-packed political painting on a wall on Leeds Road commemorates the January 1893 founding of one of the most important political groupings of the 20th century – the Independent Labour Party or ILP.

The ILP paradoxically predated the Labour Party proper by seven years. Its first meeting, held near here at the Bradford Labour Institute, was presided over by Keir Hardie, the first-ever Labour MP. Members debated about how the then-powerful Liberal Party wouldn't support working-class candidates, even though the law had changed in 1884 to allow more ordinary workers to vote, and so at the 1895 general election the ILP put up 28 candidates. They won only 44,325 votes, a failure that saw Hardie and Co. establish in London in 1900 'a distinct Labour group in Parliament' – the Labour Representation Committee, later renamed the Labour Party that we know today. It had no leader, but James Ramsay MacDonald was elected secretary. In 1924 he became the first Labour prime minister. Just to complicate things, the ILP remained as a left-wing adjunct to the main party until 1975.

Despite the ILP's leading place in the long road to socialism, some of those associated with the party down the years now appear a little suspect. Philip Snowden, chairman 1903–06, amazed Emmeline Pankhurst by opposing women having the vote, despite being a Labour Cabinet minister. Ramsay MacDonald, so important in the early years, presided in 1931 over the biggest split in Labour's history – 'the great betrayal', as future Labour prime minister Clement Attlee put it – when he disbanded his own Labour government to form a National government with the previously hated Tories and Liberals. And then there was Oswald Mosley, the 'cad and wrong 'un' as Tory PM Stanley Baldwin described him, who left the Tories to join the ILP in 1924 and later became leader of the British Union of Fascists.

INDEPENDENT LABOUR PARTY

SOCIALISM THE HOPE OF THE WORLD

CELEBRATING THE CENTENARY OF THE FORMATION OF THE INDEPENDENT LABOUR PARTY AT BRADFORD JAN 13th 1893

THERE IS NO WEAL SAVE COMMONWEAL

**Address** The mural is on the side of the Bradford Playhouse, 4 Chapel Street, Bradford, BD1 5DL | **Getting there** Just north of the A 6181, 300 yards north of Bradford Interchange station; bus 72 Pulse or 608 | **Hours** Accessible 24 hours | **Tip** Visit the well-stocked independent Bradford Mechanics' Institute Library at 76 Kirkgate, the successor to the sadly demolished Bradford Mechanics' Institute, which itself was one of a large number of similar northern establishments founded in early Victorian times to educate the working classes.

# 16 __ A Revolution in Industry
*Once the largest silk factory in the world*

Nothing signifies the enduring legacy of Yorkshire's industrial past more emphatically than sleek, brick, Lombardian mill towers dominating the landscape, and one of the greatest is at Lister's Mill in Bradford.

The mill was built in 1838 for Samuel Cunliffe Lister (later Lord Masham). It was soon employing 11,000 people, mostly women, as the biggest cloth mill in the country and the largest silk mill in the world. Lister had invented the Lister Nip Comb which allowed the different types of raw wool to be separated and straightened mechanically before being spun into yarn. The company became the first textile mill in the world to completely mechanise silk and velvet manufacturing.

Things didn't always go smoothly. An epic strike began on 9 December, 1890 when the firm reduced pay for weavers, pickers, spoolers and winders, blaming deteriorating conditions in the textile markets. To the workers' astonishment, the bosses even claimed staff had been paid too much. Lister's threatened a lock-out if workers did not accept their terms and by the end of March 1891 all 5,000 workers were out. As the workers were not unionised, and had no strike fund, the women went with their children across the North collecting donations. Threats of bailiffs and evictions saw the strike collapse. A political response saw the Bradford Labour Union form, and the Independent Labour Party created in the city in 1893.

Into the 20th century, work of the highest order continued apace. Lister's Mill supplied velvet for the Coronation of George V in 1911, made silk for parachutes during World War II, and produced velvet curtains for the White House in 1976. But foreign competition and changing industrial patterns then saw manufacturing decline, until Lister's Mill closed in 1992. Dereliction followed but Urban Splash regenerated it and the complex is now used for offices and accommodation.

**Address** Patent Street, Bradford, BD9 5BE | **Getting there** The mill is 200 yards north of the A 6177 and 400 yards west of the Keighley Road; bus 620, 621, A 6, A 8 or A 52 to Lilycroft Road then a five-minute walk | **Hours** Viewable from the outside only | **Tip** The mill hasn't been left untouched. The most remarkable new features are the rooftop duplex pods made of zinc that come with their own private outdoor terrace.

# 17 __ Saltaire Workers' Houses

*A flavour of a mighty model village*

One of the sights easiest on the eye in the self-contained model industrial village of Saltaire is this stretch of gorgeous Italianate houses. They were built in the mid-19th century according to the wishes of Titus Salt, a highly successful entrepreneur who built not just a textile mill, Salts Mill, which opened on 20 September, 1853, his 50th birthday, but the village around it: Saltaire. The name combined his own and the adjacent River Aire. The houses were of the highest quality, for Salt believed the workers deserved the best.

Salt and Saltaire prospered through trade in worsted cloth, a fine smooth yarn spun from combed wool, that made Bradford into a great industrial and commercial metropolis. Trade exploded at the beginning of the 19th century thanks to the new machines. The mill owners now enjoyed increased productivity and bigger profits, even though for the traditional workers the new power looms made their skills redundant.

Saltaire was revolutionary. Titus Salt wanted to eradicate the miserable working conditions of the day, remove the lack of sanitation, improve the meagre wages, and eliminate the poor health of the workers with their low life expectancy. The new village contained 22 streets, 850 houses and covered 25 acres. The first residents lived rent-free on an allowance of 7s. 6d. per week, with married couples allowed 5s. extra. There was a congregational chapel, which fitted in with Salt's non-conformist Christianity and catered for those unable to walk as far as the United Reform Church. Salt rewarded his employees, hiring three trains in 1857 so that he could take around 2,500 of them to the Great Art Treasures exhibition in Manchester.

The textile mill closed in February 1986, but the entrepreneur Jonathan Silver restored Salt's Mill as a cultural, retail and commercial centre. Saltaire became a World Heritage Site in 2001.

**Address** Alexandra Square, Bradford, BD18 3HD | **Getting there** Saltaire is on the A657, less than a mile west of Shipley station; train from Bradford Interchange to Shipley station; bus 60, 622, 662 or 675 from Bradford Interchange | **Hours** Accessible 24 hours | **Tip** Ideally you need to spend the day exploring the model village and taking in all its riches, particularly the mill as well as the almshouses. Start off at the Visitor Centre and pick up a leaflet.

# 18___Doncaster's Winning Post
*'I gotta horse'*

If horse racing be the sport of kings, then Doncaster is one of the princes of racecourses. Races have been held in the town since the 16th century, even though they were almost stymied in 1600 when the town authorities tried to nip such practices in the bud due to the number of ruffians attending. According to jockey Jason Weaver, who rode more than a thousand winners: 'There are not many fairer courses than Doncaster, which is a lovely, virtually flat, galloping track. It's beautifully smooth to ride; a good, solid test of a horse.'

Doncaster is home to one of the greatest flat races: the St Leger, the world's oldest classic, around which a four-day festival takes place every September. The St Leger was first raced in 1776 nearby, on Cantley Common, thanks to the promotion of Colonel Anthony St Ledger. It moved to this site, Town Moor, 10 years later, in the days when horse-racing also included cock-fighting at one aristocratic end, and three-card tricksters and pea and thimble riggers at the other. There were also occasional bouts of horse-nobbling. In 1829, the cavalry had to be summoned here to round up 'an army of the scum of England'; they've gone now.

In 1909, the racecourse was the setting for Britain's first aviation festival. The crowds couldn't believe that the fearless aviators could get these 'crates' to rise. A replica of the Bleriot monoplane from that festival can be seen at the South Yorkshire Aircraft Museum. Sadly, many of those pilots died in accidents elsewhere over the next few years. In 1992, Doncaster staged the first-ever Sunday horse-racing meeting in Britain. More than 20,000 people turned up, despite the absence of on-course betting.

The course also stages the first and last turf meetings of the flat season, although it no longer provides a regular home for legendary tipster Prince Monolulu and his infamous cry 'I gotta horse'.

**Address** Bawtry Road, Doncaster, DN4 5HH, +44 (0)1302 304200, www.doncaster-racecourse.co.uk | **Getting there** The racecourse is extremely visible and lies near the junction of the A 18 and A 638; a shuttle bus service runs between the racecourse and Doncaster Interchange station | **Hours** Intermittently, when racing is on – check website for details | **Tip** Think the horses aren't wild enough? Head east of the racecourse and over the M 18 to Yorkshire Wildlife Park, a centre for conservation and welfare with more than 400 animals and 70 different species including tigers, leopards and polar bears, although they don't race, well, not officially.

# 19 Four-Minute Warning Site
## *Defence is the best form of attack*

The people of Britain can sleep safely in their beds thanks to this obscure RAF base on Snod Hill in the North Yorks Moors. Since Fylingdales opened in 1963, it has been the home of an early warning system against ballistic missiles and the first line of defence against impending nuclear devastation. It also detects and tracks orbiting objects, including other countries' spy satellites, and reaches into space for 3,000 nautical miles in all directions, able to pick out objects as small as an alien apple.

Fylingdales' Latin motto is Vigilamus – 'We are watching' and management claim it has 'quietly performed a vital role of helping to keep the peace'. The plant employs some 80 armed forces personnel plus 80 military police, 200 civilian staff and contractors. It was built at the height of the nuclear stand-off between the West and the Soviet Union in 1963, and its existence gave rise to the idea of the four-minute warning – the time Fylingdales, and its sister stations in Greenland and Alaska, would have given governments to respond to missile attack.

For decades the site was infamous for its three giant golf balls that stunned unsuspecting drivers and became an unlikely tourist attraction. Coach tours would leave Dracula behind in Whitby and drive past, turn on the radio, and indulge in the interference caused by the radars. Sadly, the golf balls were scrapped in 1992 to be replaced by 'Solid State Phased Array Radar' – a giant pyramid, in English.

Cynics say Fylingdales is actually run by a foreign power – the USA. Although the land on which the base sits is owned by the Ministry of Defence, the equipment is owned and maintained by the US Defense Department and the plant is part of the US Space Surveillance Network. And no, Donald Trump never visited – officially. Meanwhile, its record at picking up noises from aliens has been non-existent – officially.

Address Unnamed Road, Fylingdales, YO18 7NT, +44 (0)1751 467217, www.raf.mod.uk |
Getting there Head north along the A 169 from Pickering towards Goathland | Hours
Accessible from the outside only, for obvious reasons | Tip If heading to this bizarre facility
from the south, keep heading north to Goathland, the village forever locked in the 1960s of
policemen armed only with a clip round the ear, thanks to the gentle crime drama *Heartbeat*.

# 20_Anne Lister, Shibden Hall

*The house that Jack built*

Shibden Hall is a charming manor house with the usual black-and-white timbered frontage and it's set in delicious woodland a few miles north of Halifax. Nobody ever went there but now coachloads arrive thanks to the recent *Gentleman Jack* TV show in which the ubiquitous Suranne Jones (*Coronation Street, Scott & Bailey*) stars as the early 19th-century house owner Anne Lister, often described as the first modern lesbian.

The series was inspired by the books written by feminist historian Jill Liddington, and it tells of Anne Lister's ambition to restore the estate she has inherited from her uncle on her aunt's death in 1836. The income she drew from the tenants, along with her shares in the new local canal companies, allowed her the freedom to live as she pleased. She had a 'masculine appearance', they said, dressed entirely in black decades before Lou Reed, and acted in a way that was just not 'ladylike', such as owning a coal mine. It earned her the nickname 'Gentleman Jack'.

Lister was a staunch Anglican and, this might disappoint some, remained a Tory, keen on defending the privileges of the land-owning aristocracy. Her diaries contain 7,720 pages and more than five million words, much of it in code, based on algebra and Greek, Samuel Pepys-style, and wasn't deciphered until the 1930s.

Shibden Hall was built in the 1420s and remained in the Lister family from 1610 to the 1920s. It is set in 80 acres of woodland and features cascades, pools, tunnels and fruit gardens. There is a boating lake, miniature railway and, as of now, an admission charge for the house. Brontë experts believe the hall and its rambling grounds were the model for Thrushcross Grange, home of the Lintons, in Emily Brontë's *Wuthering Heights*. On account of its recent fame it has been used for other filming, such as Mike Leigh's 2018 political drama, *Peterloo*.

**Address** Lister's Road, Halifax, HX3 6XG, +44 (0)1422 352246,
www.museums.calderdale.gov.uk | **Getting there** A 58, two miles north-east of Halifax
station; train to Halifax station and a 25-minute uphill walk; a 20-minute walk (also
uphill!) from Halifax bus station | **Hours** Mon–Fri 10am–5pm, Sat & Sun 11am–5pm |
**Tip** There is much else to do besides the hall in the extensive grounds: woodland trails, a
miniature railway, pitch and putt and a boating lake. There is also a carriage museum in the
17th-century barn.

# 21__Gibbet of Halifax

*Tortuous topper tells of 'Hell, Hull and Halifax'*

More than 50 felons were executed under the primitive guillotine that was erected here in Halifax in the 16th century. The gibbet was a popular alternative to beheading by axe or sword, and was used by the lord of the manor against any thief caught with stolen goods to the value of 13½d. or more. The ruling was simple and effective: 'If a felon be taken within their liberty of the local Forest of Hardwick, having confessed to the crime, they shall after three market days be taken to the gibbet and there have his head cut off from his body.'

Suspects were detained by the lord of the manor's bailiff, who would then summon a local jury. However, if the condemned managed to escape from the confines of the forest he could not legally be brought back to face punishment. At least two men cheated the executioner in this way, but one of them, Lacy, returned to Halifax after seven years, was caught and got the chop.

Although decapitation was a fairly common method of execution in England, particularly for traitors, Halifax was unusual in having such a machine that was used to behead petty criminals until the mid-17th century. Although there were nearly a hundred such gibbets nationwide in mediaeval times, what was unusual about Halifax was that the custom lingered on there for so long after it had been abandoned elsewhere.

By 1650, public opinion had changed, and Oliver Cromwell's Commonwealth banned the use of the gibbet for petty theft, condemning the practice as 'part of ancient ritual to be jettisoned along with all the old feasts and celebrations of the mediaeval world and the Church of Rome'. The structure was dismantled but the stone base was later discovered and this replica was erected on the site in 1974. Nearby is a plaque with the names of those decapitated here. Fortunately, the new gibbet does not have the means of beheading people.

**Address** Junction of Bedford Street North and Gibbet Street, Halifax, HX1 4DB | **Getting there** Take the A 58 north, past Calderdale College. However, Gibbet Street goes over the busy road and beware that Halifax is misery to drive round, so best park and walk; bus 532 or TS 3. | **Hours** Accessible 24 hours | **Tip** Two miles west of Halifax, off the A 646, just before the suburb of Friendly (really) is the village of Warley and the Warley Museum, probably the smallest museum in the world, given that it's housed in a phone booth.

# 22 The Piece Hall of Halifax

*Handsome hall for keeping the piece*

Breathtaking, awesome and enormous, the Piece Hall is a Classical palace that spells wealth, ambition and pride – the pride of Yorkshire's most important trade: wool. The Piece Hall was created in the 1770s when the increase in the wool trade brought about by the Industrial Revolution saw a move away from small producers and traders. The first cloth hall, where business spilled out onto the street, was now inadequate. So in April 1774 an advert appeared in the *Leeds Mercury* announcing plans to establish a new hall 'for the purpose of depositing and exposing to sale the WORSTED and WOOLLEN GOODS manufactured in this town and neighbourhood'.

The architect, either Samuel or John Hope – no one's sure – was probably aided by the better-known John Carr who was also responsible for the equally impressive Crescent in Buxton. They ruled out a circular building on such a sloping site, instead choosing a huge rectangular structure in the Romanesque style built around a courtyard. Arcades and colonnades gave the venture grace and gravitas. To overcome the slope, the structure is a storey higher on the east side, while the north and south sides taper away.

The Piece Hall opened on New Year's Day 1779. Merchants and buyers could now go inside to inspect pieces of woollen and worsted cloth, 30 yards in length, woven on a handloom, brought by packhorse, stored and shown off in numbered rooms, the name of the manufacturer displayed on the window. Change came in 1868 when the Corporation bought the place for a wholesale market hall. Disaster loomed in 1971 when the businesses were dispersed. Demolition was only quashed by one vote at the council. Further restoration took place this century to make the building a tourist attraction and centre for craft outlets.

The hall was featured in the much-loved local brass band film *Brassed Off*.

**Address** Westgate, Halifax, HX1 1RE, +44 (0)1422 525200, www.thepiecehall.co.uk |
**Getting there** Driving around Halifax is not for the faint-hearted as the council has turned
it into a nightmare. The Piece Hall is near the railway and bus stations. | **Hours** Sun–Thu
10am–11pm, Fri & Sat 10am–midnight | **Tip** Fittingly for a Classical-style institution,
there is a very popular museum nearby called Eureka, one of the best aimed at children in
the country.

# 23___ Wainhouse Tower

*World's tallest folly – no mistake*

Looming over Halifax is this 275-foot tower. It's not just the loftiest building in the borough, but remarkably the tallest folly in the world. Even more remarkably, it was erected between 1871 and 1875 as a slight. There was a long-standing feud between neighbour landowners, Sir Henry Edwards and John Edward Wainhouse. Edwards had boasted that he had the most private estate in the area, one that no one could see into, so Wainhouse built up and up, as high as he could. The first viewing platform was 369 steps up; the second a further 405 steps, and so Edwards' claims of privacy were now in tatters.

Wainhouse sold the mill to his works manager in 1874, but the latter refused to pay the cost of the chimney's construction, so Wainhouse kept the tower for himself, to be used as an observatory. Isaac Booth was the first architect, but he was soon replaced by a Richard Swarbrick Dugale who created the elaborate galleries and the corona dome. The tower was finally complete on 9 September, 1875 at a cost of £14,000 (equivalent to more than a million pounds in today's prices).

Wainhouse described his handiwork as a 'general astronomical and physical laboratory'. But it really did have a use – as a chimney for the horrendous pollution of Wainhouse's dye works. It was meant to be linked to the factory through an underground duct, but that feature was rarely used. Cleverly, the tower's height satisfied the Smoke Abatement Act of 1870, which required chimneys to waft smoke way out of the valleys. This was just as well, for chemical works coated Halifax in thick smog, blocking out sunlight, leaving the area covered in soot and sulphur dioxide.

The tower was used as a lookout during World War II. It was shut in 2006 because of safety problems and access is now limited. In 2011 the Huffington Post named the tower among the Top Ten follies in the country.

**Address** 9 Wakefield Gate, King Cross, Halifax, HX3 0HB, +44 (0)1422 288001, www.calderdale.gov.uk | **Getting there** Easily visible, of course, and by the junction of the A 646 and A 58 to the west of Halifax centre; bus 532, NH 7 or TA 1 | **Hours** All hours from the outside; bank holidays 10am – 4pm | **Tip** Head a mile east to the Shay, home of quality non-league side FC Halifax Town. There, an unusual oddity is that the roof of the Skircoat stand used to keep out the rain at Manchester City's Hyde Road Ground, a location that the top European club of today vacated back in 1923.

# 24__Bettys Tea Rooms
*'Ooh Betty!'*

The very name 'Bettys' (no apostrophising) summons up images of polite, eager-to-please waitresses in impeccable uniforms serving men with Ronald Colman moustaches and ladies in white gloves and hats à la Maud Grimes from Corrie.

Harrogate's Bettys is the flagship outlet of the most famous and best-loved old-fashioned tea rooms in the country. Bettys is 'traditional'; in other words, the tea is properly brewed in a teapot rather than thrown into a paper cup for a tenth of a second by a Barista annoyed you haven't ordered a huge flat white Frappe with hazelnut and marshmallow topping. And it's not just the tea: patrons luxuriate in bountiful, superb sandwiches stuffed with cucumber and salmon expertly crafted by a triangular machine, complemented by pâtisseries, fancies and dainty cakes.

Why 'Bettys'? No one knows. It sounds reassuringly British, yet it was founded by a Swiss man, Frederick Belmont, in July 1919 on Cambridge Crescent, Harrogate, later moving here. Belmont had arrived in London in 1907 as Fritz Bützer. He had lost the details of the address he had to find. All he knew was that it sounded like 'Bratwurst'. Unable to speak a word of English, he spent his first night in the waiting room of Bradford station. In the city of wool, he found work as a confectioner, eventually settling in the spa town of Harrogate as Frederick Belmont, 'Chocolate Specialist'.

In the 1920s, Bettys expanded into York, confectionery capital of Britain, home of Terry's and Rowntree's. Now there are six outlets. Another is in Harrogate, one in Ilkley, one in Northallerton and two now in York. Wisely, they refuse to expand out of Yorkshire, probably with the horrors of Pâtisserie Valerie in mind. In 1962, Bettys merged with Taylors of Harrogate, purveyors of quality tea, as famously drunk by Chancellor of the Exchequer Rishi Sunak in 2020 on the eve of the virus outbreak.

**Address** 1 Parliament Street, Harrogate, HG1 2QU, +44 (0)1423 814070, www.bettys.co.uk | **Getting there** A 61, just west of Harrogate train station and south-west of Harrogate bus station; bus 32, A 2 flyer or X6a | **Hours** Daily 9am–6pm | **Tip** Explore the streets around Bettys that constitute the Montpellier Quarter. They are filled with more than 50 independent high-class shops.

# 25_ Whodunit Author Hideout

*Right thriller for thriller writer*

Just where *is* Britain's leading mystery thriller writer? That was the gripping story that had the nation enthralled in 1926. Agatha Christie had simply disappeared. It turned out it was her husband, Archie Christie, wot did it. The cad had revealed that he was in love with a Nancy Neele and wanted a divorce. The couple quarrelled and on 3 December, 1926 Archie stormed out of their *des res* in Sunningdale, Berkshire to hob-nob with his mistress in Surrey. Agatha was so mortified she decided to disappear, having made sure she kissed her sleeping daughter, Rosalind, first.

To turn the domestic into a full-blown whodunit, Agatha Christie, in best Agatha Christie fashion, cleverly abandoned her Morris Cowley car near Guildford. But were there any clues, officer? Just a letter for her secretary saying she was going to Yorkshire. A huge manhunt followed, but no solution could be found. The Tory home secretary, William Joynson-Hicks, whose sole achievement to date had been to beat Winston Churchill in a Manchester by-election, put pressure on the police. Even Dorothy L. Sayers, one of Christie's writer peers, was drawn into the search, to no avail.

There was only one thing to do: call for Sherlock Holmes or rather the latter's creator, Arthur Conan Doyle. A believer in the occult, he took one of Christie's discarded gloves to a medium. Even that didn't work, but time did. Eleven days after her disappearance, Christie was identified as a guest here at the Old Swan hotel in Harrogate, registered as Mrs Teresa Neele (sic) of Cape Town, not that her readers had managed to work that out.

Why did she do it, asked the Poirots of the day? Christie didn't say, but the smart money was on a nervous breakdown. Some unkindly suggested it was all a publicity stunt, perhaps to make the police think her husband had killed her. Dorothy L. Sayers based her novel *Unnatural Death* on the tale.

**Address** Old Swan Hotel, Swan Road, Harrogate, HG1 2SR, +44 (0)1423 500055, www.classiclodges.co.uk | **Getting there** Swan Road is just to the west of the A61, Ripon Road, and just north of the Royal Pump Room Museum; train to Harrogate railway station; bus 7, 36, A2 or X52 | **Hours** Usual hotel hours – check website for details | **Tip** For another, more elemental, mystery, head 10 miles north-west to the weird and wonderful formation of Brimham Rocks, a stunning collection of stone oddities.

# 26_ Turkish Baths

*Ornate Ottoman décor washed with healing waters*

Mesmerising proto-geometric patterns, serpentine mosaics and glorious azure tiles laced with lapis lazuli. These will soothe the eyes and inspire the mind while you lie back on the *gobek tasi* heated marble slab ready to take the heavenly Harrogate waters.

Turkish baths were once ubiquitous; now they are a rarity, but Harrogate's have helped make the town one of Britain's leading spa resorts, and it was recently named the best place in Britain for working from home. Harrogate's first mineral spring was discovered in 1571 by William Slingsby who claimed that water from the Tewit Well possessed properties similar to those found in the springs of the Belgian town of Spa. As word spread that the waters could cure scurvy, epilepsy and ulcers, wealthy visitors made Harrogate the 'Queen of Inland Watering Places'.

Around the baths a fashionable town grew. There were assembly rooms, libraries and theatres. Famous visitors arrived. Daniel Defoe wrote in 1724 of how 'coming to the Wells to drink the waters was a mere Matter of Custom; some drink, more do not, and few drink physically. But company and Diversion is the main business'. By 1860 there were over 10,000 annual visitors to Harrogate, but not everyone was euphoric. Charles Dickens wrote how 'Harrogate is the queerest place with the strangest people in it, leading the oddest lives of dancing, newspaper reading and dining.'

These Turkish baths opened in 1897 as one of a huge number of facilities in the Royal Baths complex. Treatments included a medicinal waters dispensary, hydrotherapy departments, mud baths and steam rooms. It also has a Calidarium (hot), Laconium (hottest), plunge pool, steam room and Frigidarium. Interest in such spas declined with the advent of the NHS, which gave ailing individuals more scientific choices. Now there's a revival in such establishments, if only for the novelty value.

**Address** Parliament Street, Harrogate, HG1 2WH, +44 (0)1423 556746,
www.turkishbathsharrogate.co.uk | **Getting there** The baths are just off the A 61, half a mile
north of the railway station and a 20-minute walk from the bus station. | **Hours** Mon – Fri
9.45am – 8.30pm, Sat & Sun 9am – 8.30pm | **Tip** Where else to go after a Turkish bath than
a short walk west to the Royal Pump Room museum with its displays on Harrogate's former
role as England's premier spa?

# 27 __ Cabinet of Curiosities
*'To cure the soul by means of the senses …'*

Inside this magnificent Victorian-styled shop is a veritable treasure trove of euphoric enchantment. The Cabinet of Curiosities is decked out like an apothecary's druggists, which is exactly what it was 200 years ago when the incorrigible Branwell Brontë, the famous sisters' mad, bad and dangerous brother, would frequent it to pick up his fix of laudanum, the fashionable drug of the day.

Laudanum is a tincture of opium – 10 per cent of the drug dissolved in alcohol. It was used as a painkiller and to ease coughs, rheumatism, and what were described as 'women's troubles'. Babies were given it to send them to sleep. Every home had a bottle of Collis Browne's cure-all mixture. According to Samuel Taylor Coleridge, 'it gave repose, a spot of enchantment, a green spot of fountain and flowers and trees in the very heart of a waste of sands'.

Branwell Brontë toked himself to death at the age of 31. He was spurred on by his hero, Thomas de Quincey, author of *Confessions of an English Opium-Eater*. As far as Branwell was concerned, if the 'opium-eater' could take 53 ounces of laudanum in one day, then it surely could not harm him to take three, and unlike with alcohol it was not immediately noticeable that one's demeanour had changed. But Branwell drank heavily as well, at the Black Bull opposite, and expired in 1848 a few months after the publication of sister Emily's remarkable *Wuthering Heights* which, according to some misogynist commentators, Branwell wrote and Emily stole off him.

The owners of the Cabinet of Curiosities bought the shop 30 years ago and restored it to its former glory by buying up antique shop fittings and units they had salvaged from chemists, grocery shops and museums. Inspired by the 'wonder-rooms' of Renaissance Europe, offerings include handmade candles – the Damson Plum, Rose & Patchouli are particular favourites – and soaps made out of coffee, lemongrass and goat's milk.

**Address** 84 Main Street, Haworth, BD22 8DP, +44 (0)1535 646830, www.the-curiosity-society.myshopify.com | **Getting there** Main Street is literally *the* main street in Haworth, tourist central, with many car parks and is well-signposted off the B 6142 | **Hours** Mon–Fri 10am–5pm, Sat & Sun 10am–5.30pm | **Tip** The Black Bull pub opposite is Haworth's best known hostelry and central to the town's history. Here the fiery late 18th-century preacher William Grimshaw chased out church dodgers with a whip. Nowadays gullible patrons are directed to 'Branwell Brontë's chair'.

# 28_Railway Children Railway

*Travel back to the golden age of steam*

This gorgeous picturesque heritage steam railway from the golden age of rail travel is officially the Keighley and Worth Valley Railway. It runs for five stunningly picturesque miles through the heart of Brontë Country around Haworth, and was used generously and gloriously as the railway featured in the 1970 family tear-jerker film, The Railway Children.

In 1861 John McLandsborough, a civil engineer, went to Haworth to visit Charlotte Brontë and was amazed to discover there was no railway line. He proposed a route and convinced local mill owners it would service the vibrant local woollen industry as well as shipping huge loads of coal. It opened in 1867. During the opening ceremony, a train became stuck twice and had to be split in two.

Nearly a hundred years later the line was shut as part of the Beeching-Marples cuts. A preservation society was soon formed and the line reopened in June 1968. The route is not an easy ride; there is a steep gradient from Keighley. These days commuters, happy to travel at a leisurely but lovely pace, come down from Keighley, take the train, preferably one of the steam versions, to the southern terminus at Oxenhope and then transfer to one of the most scenic bus routes in the country, to Hebden Bridge where they can pick up national rail.

The line played a central role in The Railway Children starring Jenny Agutter, Bernard Cribbins, Dinah Sheridan and Sally Thomsett, used because it was one the few of its kind that had a tunnel. But it has also been used in a remarkable range of productions: Last of the Summer Wine, Pink Floyd's The Wall, Peaky Blinders, a recent remake of Swallows and Amazons, and predictably, but effectively, a dramatisation of the 1963 Great Train Robbery.

Regular events are held on the railway, including afternoon tea on the White Rose Pullman Dining Train and the Beer and Music Festival.

**Address** Keighley & Worth Valley Railway, The Railway Station, Haworth, BD22 8NJ, +44 (0)1535 645214, www.kwvr.co.uk | **Getting there** The station is just off the B 6142 | **Hours** See website for details of events and to book tickets | **Tip** Oxenhope at the southern terminus is a delightful village, which holds many festivals and shows including an annual straw race in which competitors have to carry a bale of straw for more than two miles between five pubs and down a pint in each.

# 29 Brontë's Shooting Range

*Novel way of redecorating the church wall*

The Reverend Patrick Brunty, better known by his altered surname, Brontë, Perpetual Curate of Haworth 1820–61, would wake up in the morning, pick up his flintlock pistols, and fire them out of the window at the wall of his church, St Michael's and All Angels. The pock marks can still be seen on the western side.

It sounds bizarre and drastic, but there was method to his madness. The good cleric, father of the world-renowned Brontë sisters, was fearful of a local uprising by the Luddites, the violent saboteurs who went around smashing machines that they claimed were putting them out of work, as Charlotte Brontë captured in her 1849 novel Shirley. Brontë had worked in areas beset by such trouble and was wary as a cleric of being targeted, so he slept with a pair of loaded pistols by his bed. His choice of firearm was dramatic. Flintlock pistols, once loaded, couldn't be unloaded. Rather than leave the loaded guns lying around each morning, he would discharge them by shooting out of his bedroom window at the church wall.

The Reverend's residence was the parsonage, now one of the most popular literary museums in the country. Alongside is the rambling graveyard, permanent home to some 40,000 people. Under the graveyard in the Brontës' days ran the water pipe into which, it was later discovered, remnants of the Haworth dead would seep, probably one of the reasons why the average life expectancy in the village was 24.

Revd Brontë insisted that improvements in sanitation be made and he was helped by the Board of Health's Benjamin Babbage (son of the computing pioneer Charles Babbage). It was too late to save his great writer daughters, whose tragic early deaths came from diseases exacerbated by the tainted water. When each Brontë daughter died, their coffin was carried into the church from the parsonage garden through the gate of death, still a morbid attraction.

**Address** St Michael and All Angels, 125 Main Street, Haworth, BD22 8DR, +44 (0)1535 648464, www.haworthchurch.co.uk | **Getting there** Arrive on the B 6142, park and walk. Only locals should try to drive up the ridiculously steep Main Street. The station is on a heritage line. | **Tip** Take in the Brontë Parsonage Museum, one of the most famous literary establishments in the country, where the Brontës lived, wrote and died.

# 30_ Wuthering Heights Pub
*Book a place for a visit to the landlord*

Unsurprisingly, the pub wasn't called the Wuthering Heights before the novel was published in 1847, but what a good choice of name. If it wasn't for Emily Brontë's one-off novel, Haworth would be just another picturesque hilly Yorkshire village. Instead, thousands of visitors descend daily, particularly in the summer, as it's a bit parky at the other end of the year, and even from as far away as Japan.

Wuthering Heights is one of the least-read famous novels in English literature, many put off by the labyrinthine familial relationships and the lengthy passages devoted to Cathy's emotional ramblings. Millions know it mostly because of the laughably bad 1939 Hollywood film starring Laurence Olivier as the brooding Heathcliff and Merle Oberon as Cathy. But it is a captivating read, particularly for the passages that segue into the supernatural, such as when Lockwood, the narrator, forced to stay the night at the eponymous house due to a snowstorm, drifts in and out of a nightmare, knocks his knuckles through the glass, stretches an arm out to seize a branch that's been bashing his window and finds his fingers closing on those of a little, ice-cold hand!

The locale is filled with Wuthering Heights locations; ironically Haworth never gets a mention in the book, for it is featured as the fictitious Gimmerton. Yet few visitors get to this pub, probably because it's a good mile west of the main drag and the Brontë Parsonage Museum. Nevertheless, there's a delightful walk to be had from the museum to the hostelry through the woods at the edge of the bleak moor, hanging a right by the reservoir to the hamlet of Stanbury. After a jar or two the *flâneur* might want to get back the easy way to Haworth proper. There is an hourly bus that quaintly stops at only one spot on the road, regardless of which way it's going.

Oh, and there's that song as well of the same name.

**Address** Main Street, Stanbury, near Haworth, BD22 0HB, +44 (0)1535 643332, www.thewutheringheights.co.uk | **Hours** Mon–Thu 4–10pm, Fri, Sat & Sun noon–11pm | **Tip** Plan in advance a walk out from the Parsonage Museum onto the wilds of the moors (summer only) and a long but rewarding trip to the Brontë Waterfall, the Brontë chair and the ruins of Top Withens, which some believe was the inspiration for *Wuthering Heights* itself.

# 31 Heavenly? Hebden Bridge
*Rural Ruritania*

Is it the way the rivers, streams and becks weft and wind around the canal? Is it the perfect union of stone and woodland? Is it the Cinema Paradiso on the main street? Is it the much-loved perfectly formed Trades Club music venue and nearby Little Theatre? Is it the gaggle of puddle geese that brazenly cross the busy Halifax Road while honking at the drivers? Or is it all of that?

Hebden Bridge, half-way between Manchester and Leeds, and half-way between being a big village and a small town, seems too good to be true. Historically it was a typical textile town using the waters of the River Calder – 'the hardest worked river in England', according to local poet Ted Hughes. Its nickname was 'Trouser Town'. But when the cloth industry began to decline in the 1960s many people moved out and were replaced by those seeking alternative lifestyles who took over dirt cheap properties that are now massively overpriced. The demographic change became complete. By the 1980s, Hebden Bridge had become the lesbian capital of Britain, jokingly twinned with the equally woke Chorlton-cum-Hardy of Manchester. Imaginatively, the MP is nearly always Tory, even though admitting publicly to voting blue would mean instant social ostracism and the most pressing political pastime is predictably Palestine.

Tradition is all here: no chain stores, Starbucks or McDonald's are allowed, the high street is lined with organic, vegetarian and fair trade cafés and restaurants, and the cultural facilities, including some very popular pub quizzes, are remarkable for so small a place. For those of an outgoing nature it is the glorious countryside that draws folk to the wooded splendour of Hardcastle Crags and Mytholm, washed by the waters of the Rochdale Canal, the River Calder, Hebden Water and Colden Water, which sadly occasionally combine to create some of the worst flooding in the country.

**Address** HX7 | **Getting there** Train is best on the slow line between Leeds and Manchester Victoria as the roads get very clogged and are always being repaired | **Hours** Accessible 24 hours | **Tip** There are a bewildering number of pubs here but two stand out. A mile west of the centre on the A 646, the main road running through Hebden Bridge, is the cooperatively owned Fox & Goose, down-home, beer-minded, and featuring a popular Monday night quiz and occasional you-can-all-join-in folk session on a Sunday night. A half-mile further west is the Stubbing Wharf, cruelly traduced by Ted Hughes but perfectly situated on the canal, with excellent food and a Thursday night quiz.

# 32 Heptonstall's Abandoned Church

*And the walls came tumbling down*

Mesmerising, mysterious and magical is the sight of this dead church in Heptonstall, the most atmospheric of villages. Only the walls stand at the abandoned church of St Thomas a Becket, built in 1260, the rest long vanquished by the elements. The church fell in the great storm of 1847, when the west face of the tower gave way. Some repairs followed, but the parish decided to simply let it rot away. What an excellent idea; to leave us with something like this! Certainly, Danny Boyle thought so when he chose it as a location in his 1993 televised version of the cult novel about an early 19th-century Christian sect, *Mr Wroe's Virgins*.

But that's not all. A new church, St Thomas the Apostle, was built only a few hundred yards away, creating a rare example – Westminster Abbey and St Margaret's Westminster is another – of two churches in one churchyard. Walking through is tricky, especially when the snows fall, but it is worth it, for here are the graves of the notorious coiners, counterfeiters led by 'King' David Hartley who would clip the metal from people's loose change, milling the edges to make new money. Their activities were so damaging they threatened to wreck the validity of Britain's currency. Hartley was eventually hanged near York in April 1770.

Heptonstall is the village that time forgot: 'Black village of grave-stones/The hill's collapsed skull/Whose dreams die back/Where they were born', according to local poet Ted Hughes. Even though Heptonstall is only a mile from Hebden Bridge, it is located up a heart-pumping hill with a wicked gradient. Perambulating Hepton-stall it is hard to believe that electricity has been installed or that news of Queen Victoria's accession, let alone her death, has arrived, such is the air of antiquity.

**Address** Church Street, Hebden Bridge, HX7 7NT, www.visitcalderdale.com | **Getting there** Drive to Hebden Bridge, head west a mile-and-a-half to the turning circle and then turn back, taking the Heptonstall Road, which veers uphill at the Fox and Goose pub. Continue uphill a mile to Heptonstall where the church is prominent. | **Hours** Accessible 24 hours | **Tip** A few hundred yards north stands the 1764 octagonal Methodist chapel, one of the oldest Methodist meeting halls in the country, where John Wesley frequently preached.

# 33__Sylvia Plath's Grave

*Stasis in darkness for God's lioness*

Followers come from afar – especially from America – to pay homage at the grave of this celebrated mid-20th-century poet. Sylvia Plath will always be known as the ill-fated first wife of the better-known locally born Ted Hughes, but her own work was of a similar high standard. US poet Robert Pinsky, late 20th-century poet laureate to the Library of Congress, described her poetry as 'thrashing, hyperactive, perpetually accelerated'.

Sylvia Plath was born in Boston, Massachusetts, in 1932 to a middle-class family. The premature death of her father Otto caused young Sylvia much misery and pushed her into depression. Despite excelling at school, she felt alienated from her peers. After an unsuccessful suicide bid she underwent electro-shock treatment, which provided material for her autobiographical work *The Bell Jar*, published in 1963 after her death. At Cambridge University she met Hughes. At one of their first liaisons Ted stole her earring, so Sylvia bit his cheek so hard it drew blood. Nevertheless, they were married in June 1956, but it was Ted who won all the literary plaudits while she remained mostly ignored – and distraught at his affairs.

Sylvia moved to Camden Town, London, into the house where W. B. Yeats had once lived, but during the bitterly cold winter of 1962–63 she was alone with young children in a place with no heating while Hughes did the literary circuit with his mistress. When she discovered that Hughes' lover was expecting, it proved too much. She gassed herself in February 1963, locking the two children in a bedroom with a plate of bread and butter, and glasses of milk, sealing the door to stop the gas entering. The manuscript of her last book of poetry, *Ariel*, was on the table.

Ted Hughes has never been forgiven for the cruelty he inflicted on her. Consequently, the name 'Hughes' on her gravestone here in Heptonstall often gets vandalised.

IN MEMORY
SYLVIA PLATH HUGHES
1932 – 1963
EVEN AMIDST FIERCE FLAMES
THE GOLDEN LOTUS CAN BE PLANTED

**Address** 12 Becketts Close, Heptonstall, HX7 7LJ | **Getting there** The best way of getting to Heptonstall is to head for Hebden Bridge and take the A 646 to the turning circle a mile west of the town. This allows drivers to briefly head back on themselves, but it's the only way to slip smoothly onto the Heptonstall Road at the Fox & Goose pub. | **Hours** Open daylight hours | **Tip** For a rewarding strenuous walk (or a much easier drive), head north-west past the museum along Smithwell Lane to explore Slack Top and Slack Bottom.

# 34__ Ted Hughes' Lumb Bank
*Woodland lair for wild laureate*

No writer has captured in verse the elemental, visceral West Riding landscape more vividly than Ted Hughes, poet laureate 1984–98, and this is his 'Kingdom of Elmet'.

Hughes was born in 1930 in Mytholmroyd, a sparse village a mile east of the more celebrated Hebden Bridge, which is a mile south of this isolated spot. At Cambridge he met the American writer Sylvia Plath whom he married and abused psychologically. But of his books, his *Remains of Elmet* threnody from 1979 is a homage to the ancient legends of the Kingdom of Elmet that ruled this part of Yorkshire. It was England's last Celtic stronghold, described by John Wesley as 'the most beautiful valley in England with the most barbarous people'. They've mostly gone now.

In the 19th century the area became heavily industrialised and the River Calder 'the hardest-worked in England', according to Hughes. His mentions of local places in poems are plentiful. *Remains of Elmet* celebrates the landscape and its survivors, such as the Crown Point Pensioners, with their 'Old faces, old roots / Indigenous memories / Singers of a lost kingdom', Crown Point being the very top of nearby Heptonstall village. In his letters, Hughes predictably moans about the weather: 'It's been raining and blowing and sunning all at once, all day, with the most incredible huge crowded brilliant skies'.

In 1969, Hughes bought this property, Lumb Bank, a half-derelict mill-owner's house set in gorgeous wooded countryside, 'an eyrie over the crevasse of trees and water', its official postcode the middle of nowhere. He moved in with his children and his lover, Brenda Hedden, and her children. Despite the beauty of the landscape it didn't work out and in 1974 he leased it to the Arvon Foundation, a creative writing organisation. It is now a writers' retreat with no distractions, the nearest shop or pub a tortuous walk to Heptonstall, the village that time forgot (see ch. 32).

**Address** Lumb Bank, Lumb Road, near Heptonstall, HX7 6DF, +44 (0)1422 843714, www.arvon.org | **Getting there** From Heptonstall, take the north-west road, Smithwell Lane, and then turn left onto Green Lane, but plan your journey in advance to avoid getting stuck in ditches or no through routes. Alternatively, there is a superb but difficult walk north from Hebden Bridge. | **Hours** By appointment; see the website for details of writing courses and retreats | **Tip** Plan carefully in advance a walking route, preferably from Hebden Bridge, to Heptonstall Quarry and Hell-Hole Rocks. This is one of the most breathtaking spots in Yorkshire, a gritstone quarry offering formidable climbing and an escape route cut into rocks not for the faint-hearted. Dogs love it.

# 35 __ Classic Classical Station
*But surely it's the Town Hall?*

Surely that can't be the station? It must be the Town Hall or a grand country house transported to the town. But no, it's Huddersfield railway station, one of only six Grade I-listed stations in the country. Indeed, the poet John Betjeman described it as the most splendid in the land.

Huddersfield station was built in 1847 at a time when growing northern industrial towns were determined to show their municipal ambition by building in the grand Greek Classical style with a huge central portico and colonnades stretching away as far as the eye can see … well, at least as far as the pubs at each end. Originally these were ticket offices, with one office for the Huddersfield and Manchester Railway company, the other for the Manchester & Leeds outfit. The two were great rivals and had to be forced to compromise to build the station, and so the two offices were as far apart as feasible. It's hard to believe that when the route was first proposed at a local civic meeting there was a huge row, with one man announcing: 'They have clapped us in a hole and want to keep us there!' The meeting ended in uproar after an official declared that Huddersfield 'was not worth stopping the engine for'.

Nevertheless, the setting was beautifully chosen. Many northern railway stations are sited in bizarrely obscure spots – Rochdale and Stockport for instance – but Huddersfield's opens out onto a huge public square where the buildings are mostly constructed from the same local buff sandstone. There is a clue to the remarkable architecture. The station was built on land that belonged to the Ramsden family who were connected to the monumental Wentworth Woodhouse stately home to the south-west. They insisted the station architect be their own man, James Pigott Pritchett.

The station is unusual in employing a senior pest controller – Felix – a furry figure who sleeps all day and patrols at night.

**Address** St George's Square, Huddersfield, HD1 1JB | **Getting there** Coming by rail is a good choice, as Huddersfield is a stop on the main Leeds to Manchester line. Driving around Huddersfield, like Halifax, is not for the impatient. The A 62 encircles the town like a merry-go-round you can never get off. | **Hours** Accessible 24 hours | **Tip** Huddersfield is one of those northern towns crying out for a wrecking ball to come and remove all the decrepit 1960s' concrete monstrosities and dual carriageways so that the days of civic grandeur can be revealed properly. In the meantime, head to the actual Town Hall itself, nearly a mile south of the station.

# 36 __ Emley Moor Mast
*It's got a TV eye on you*

Taller than The Shard, higher than the Eiffel Tower, at 1,084 feet the Emley Mast, halfway between Huddersfield and Barnsley, is the loftiest structure in Britain and the 24th-highest tower in the world. Designed as a tapered, cylindrical pillar by Arup, one of the most famous names in engineering, and made of reinforced concrete, it began life as a transmitting station in 1971. It takes a nervy seven minutes in the lift to get to the top for an unparalleled non-aeroplane view of the surrounding hills.

This mast is the third. The original went up in 1956 for the then novel and ground-breaking idea of independent television – TV paid for by adverts rather than by the government. The structure was improved in 1966 for another remarkable new advent: colour TV. Remarkably, in March 1969, strong winds and the accumulation of weighty ice caused the structure to collapse. The wreckage was strewn across the fields. Amazingly no one was injured, but people were without ITV for four days, so no Corrie. At least some good use was made of the collapsed tower, which was converted for use as a control tower at Huddersfield Sailing Club. An interim tower was imported from Sweden and erected by a team of Polish riggers, the only people willing to work in the winter conditions.

The current tower started to go up in 1971, built slightly to the south-east, with a ladder running the entire height containing 865 rungs. Although it is designed to withstand winds of up to 150 mph, don't tell anyone, it sways in the wind, inducing sea-sickness in the observation deck, which is placed almost near the top, where a team works, and can be reached by a non-stop lift.

In 2017 came a shock. For four years there would be two Emley Moor masts, the second needed while work was carried out on the technology of the original. The temporary mast is almost as tall as the proper tower.

**Address** Jagger Lane, Huddersfield, HD8 9TQ | **Getting there** From the M1, exit at Junction 38 and join the A637 Huddersfield Road. The mast can be easily seen. | **Hours** Viewable from the outside only | **Tip** Some five miles westwards is Castle Hill, Almondbury, setting for the remains of a late-Bronze Age hillfort and topped with the Victoria Tower, a mere stripling compared with the never-ending Emley Moor mast. It was nearly removed during World War II lest it be used as a navigational aid by German bombers.

# 37__Harold Wilson on the Go

*A statue is a long time in statuary*

Harold Wilson, born here in Huddersfield, was the most successful ever Labour prime minister, winner of four general elections. He was the great social reformer, for during his time in office, off and on between 1964 and 1976, capital punishment was abolished, homosexuality de-criminalised, abortion laws introduced, the Open University created and the Vietnam War avoided. He coined the now overused phrase: 'A week is a long time in politics', while other famous quotes of his include: 'The Labour Party is a moral crusade or it is nothing', and the magnificent 'I'm an optimist, but an optimist who carries a raincoat' (Gannex).

Wilson read modern history at Oxford where he was a member of the Liberal Party and considered one of the best students they'd ever had, becoming a don aged only 21. At the end of World War II he won the seat of Ormskirk in the 1945 Labour landslide and swiftly entered government. His accession to the Labour leadership came unexpectedly, following the alleged assassination of Hugh Gaitskell in 1963. Despite the social advances during his tenure, he was regularly lambasted as being devious, an 'unprincipled opportunist' according to Paul Foot, and his latter years were beset by paranoia – justified it turned out – that he was being bugged by the Soviets, the Richardson gang, and who knows who else, which led to a sudden retirement in 1976. On being elevated to the House of Lords he took the appellation Rievaulx, a small village in the Dales.

Appropriately enough, Tony Blair, who won three general elections, unveiled this statue in July 1999. The statue, which is by Ian Walters, is about one and a half times Wilson's physical size. Surprisingly, it omits his trademark pipe and even more surprisingly his equally identifiable Gannex raincoat, which were at the request of his wife, Mary, who wanted him to look instead like a man on the go.

**Address** St George's Square, Huddersfield, HD1 1JB | **Getting there** The square is right in front of the railway station. Don't even think about driving. | **Hours** Accessible 24 hours | **Tip** Head a short distance north to Bath Street to see one of the last Owenite Halls of Science in the country. These socialist and social meeting places were inspired by Robert Owen, one of the greatest figures in history, who 200 years ago created the co-operative movement, built Britain's first primary schools and fought for the factory acts that stopped women and children working down the mines.

# 38__ Lions of Huddersfield
*A roaring success*

Despite lying thousands of miles from the African jungle, Huddersfield abounds with some 200 lions. But don't worry. They don't bite. Indeed, they're harmless, for they are stone and adorn everything from take-aways to civic buildings.

The lions of Huddersfield were the work of a prominent local family, the Ramsdens, who ran the local manor from 1599 until 1920 when it was sold to the Corporation. They devised the lions as a symbol of strength and empire – after all, the English symbol is three lions, even though they were imported from France by Henry II. The Huddersfield Civic Society has explained that 'it's unusual for a town to have so many lions. They reflect our history; who controlled the town and the fact that people thought lions would support their civic pride.' The Civic Society arranges regular lion hunts around the streets of Huddersfield – 'binoculars, a plus' – which encourage people to take a fresh view of their town.

The best way to start the safari is in St George's Square in the centre where there are at least 25 on the grand civic buildings. One of the best known is the giant 11-foot fibreglass beast on top of Lion Chambers, natch, opposite Huddersfield Station. It replaced the original concrete one erected in 1853, which was starting to fall apart. Other leonine animals, carved in stone or wood, cast in iron or ceramic, painted and plain, can be found above doorways and on window ledges.

These lions have no airs and graces; two can be found at the Dixy Chicken takeaway, there's a shaggy gold beast on the coat of arms at the former court and a pair of elegant Art Deco lions as flag pole bearers on the former Co-op. There are 12 on a frieze by Caffè Nero, more than 20 on Estate Buildings, and a number of cubs on the wedding crests in Railway Street. Surprisingly, the local football club, the once mighty Huddersfield Town, is known as the Terriers.

**Address** Start at St George's Square | **Getting there** Start at St George's Square outside Huddersfield station | **Hours** Accessible 24 hours | **Tip** On the north-eastern edge of the town is the multi-purpose John Smith's stadium, named after the overrated beer, which is home to the rugby league outfit with the naff American name, Huddersfield Giants, and perennial football underachievers Huddersfield Town. Of the latter, there is now no one left alive who witnessed their remarkable three consecutive league titles in the 1920s, which even more remarkably marks the last time they have won any trophy.

# 39 — Fish Trail of Hull

*You batter believe it. Hull's not codding*

Whale of a time jokes aside, the scale of this street art undertaking is truly mind-yawling. Forty-one high-quality pieces of sculpture by Gordon Young have been plaiced, sorry placed, on the pavements of the Old Town to form an A–Z of fish.

The trail was slabbed out in 1992. Young created the pieces to represent the actual size of the fish and based designs on the drawings of local Victorian artist F. S. Smith. The first course is a school of 36 anchovies outside City Hall. According to the caption, the anchovy is 'a small bony fish commonly found off the coast of Peru', although to most people it is usually found in tiny cans. In contrast the ray is 10 foot. The lobster is characterised by an enlarged pair of pincers, with eight of them cut into Cornish slate, accompanied by a quotation from Lewis Carroll's Alice in Wonderland.

The icefish, so called because its blood has no haemoglobin, appears whitishly pale in colour. A shoal of tiny transparent-styled X-ray fish are etched onto glass above the Beverley Gate and there are herrings cut into the red-brick pavement along Posterngate. To honour the mackerel caught in such huge numbers locally there are plenty swimming in stone around the back of Holy Trinity Church. Dogfish, actually a small species of shark, reside alongside the catfish, the latter sadly not jumping on a pole.

There are some odd inclusions. A warty doris can be found at the corner of Castle Street and Humber Dock Street. A quid, a cousin of the salmon, is carved in Hopton Wood stone on Minerva Terrace near a viviparous blenny. Worth looking out for is the Naucrates ductor – or pilot fish – which accompany sharks, lucky things. The artist and organisers clearly had a sense of humour. Four plaice are carved in York Stone in the Market Place; the shark is outside the bank, and there's an electric eel outside the Electricity Showroom. Fin.

**Address** 79 Carr Lane, Hull, HU1 3RQ. You can download the Fish Trail from www.visithull.org/wp-content/uploads/2020/06/Fish-Trail.pdf | **Getting there** Take the A63 to the Hull Marina; bus 7, 8 simplibus, 33, 35, 35a or 55 | **Hours** Accessible 24 hours | **Tip** Easily noticeable is the Spurn Lightship in Hull Marina. Built in 1927, it spent nearly 50 years helping vessels negotiate the Humber Estuary, before being decommissioned and moved here to be a museum.

# 40 Hull's Civil War Pub

*Not so civil history*

Cities are supposed to welcome kings and queens when they plan a visit, but at Ye Olde White Harte the town's leaders met in 1642 to refuse King Charles I entry, a decision said to have been one of the triggers for the English Civil War.

The meeting took place upstairs in what is now the pub's Plotting Parlour, reached by a gorgeous period staircase. There, Sir John Hotham, governor of Hull, decided to close the town gates to stop Charles laying his hands on the huge arsenal kept within the city boundaries. When the king was unable to get his way he and his forces besieged Hull for three weeks.

Wind on a generation and Ye Old White Harte was setting for another major political meeting. A plot was hatched here to overthrow the Catholic governor of the city. The governor had been appointed by the Catholic King James II but James had just been thrown off the throne due to his religious affiliations, and replaced by his nephew and son-in-law William of Orange to ensure the monarchy was Protestant. For many years the event was celebrated as Town Taking Day.

The pub dates back to 1550 although it was almost destroyed by fire in the 19th century. It features oak panelling, inglenook fireplaces and a recess in a wall that sports a human skull. The skull is said to be that of a youth who died from a blow to the head delivered by an angry sea captain who, soused with brandy, bashed the boy on the head with the butt of his pistol, which can be seen as a fracture on the skull. The skeletal boy was placed under the staircase, and remained there undiscovered until after the 19th-century fire. An alternative story says that the skull was found in the attic during renovations in 1881 and is all that remains of a serving girl caught in a secret liaison. Just to add to the fun, the pub is haunted by four spirits, the Blue Lady the most famous.

# 41_Humber Bridge
*Ever so humber*

Golden Gate Bridge, San Francisco, be damned. The Humber Bridge, one and a half miles long, is the longest suspension bridge in the world that can be crossed by foot. It spans the river of the same name 10 miles west of Hull, linking Yorkshire with Lincolnshire via the A15. On the north side is Hessle (where bits of the bridge fell down shortly before completion); on the south, Barton-upon-Humber. An alternative route across the M62 is 24 miles west.

When the Humber Bridge opened to traffic on 24 June, 1981 it was the longest of its type in the world. It is now only the 11th longest. For decades locals had spoken of the need for such a bridge to counteract the single-carriageway roads across foggy moors. An Act was passed in 1959 but work didn't begin until July 1972.

But why a suspension bridge? The Humber Estuary has a shifting bed. It can take ships but the geology is always changing. A suspension bridge with no support piers would not obstruct vessels. Also, a tunnel would have been far more costly.

Bernard Wex submitted a design for a bridge that would last 120 years; wind tunnel testing was carried out in London. Of all the features of engineering and precise mathematics governing the structure, one of the most interesting is that the two end towers are not of the same height, but differ by 36 millimetres due to the curvature of the Earth. They are each about half the size of the Eiffel Tower.

Once opened, the road-distance between Hull and Grimsby fell by nearly 50 miles. One of the downsides is the toll, but somebody had to pay for its cost, which leapt from £28 million to £98 million. A further social problem was the tally of more than 200 incidents of people jumping off, of whom only five survived, leading to the building of a suicide barrier. In 2013 it was announced to widespread amazement that the bridge was not insured.

**Address** A 15, Barton-upon-Humber, +44 (0)1482 64716, www.humberbridge.co.uk |
**Getting there** An easy circular walk of around four miles can be started in Hessle or
Barton-upon-Humber | **Hours** Accessible 24 hours | **Tip** Eight miles east on the north
side of the Humber is the eerie waterside hamlet of Paul where the most remarkable feature
are the crazy, frightening Daleks, lofty structures that claim to be in reality the lights of
Thorngumbald Clough, which sounds even more sci-fi.

# 42 Land of Green Ginger

*Spicy name, home to England's smallest window*

This has to be the street with one of the best names in the country, an evocative improvement on what it used to be called: plain Old Beverley Street. All around is the Old Town of Hull on the west bank of the River Hull near its confluence with the Humber. Here are cobbled streets, quirky little museums, a statue of one of the greatest locals (the 17th-century poet Andrew Marvell), the ornate baroque Hepworth Arcade, which is home of Dinsdale's Joke Shop, the gastronomic delights of the former Fruit Market, and Hull Minster where the anti-slavery promoter William Wilberforce was baptised.

There are all sorts of theories as to the origins of the street's name. The spice ginger might have been sold or stored here in the Middle Ages. Maybe there was a Dutch family with the surname Lindegroen ('green lime tree') who lived here 200 years ago, giving us a *Lindegroen jonger* ('Lindegreen junior'), which later metamorphosed into the more romantic Land of Green Ginger.

The gorgeous name has attracted many tributes from the arts: novels by Winifred Holtby and Noel Langley, and a 2004 track by electro-ambient kings The Orb. Beatrix Potter's 1929 novel, *The Fairy Caravan*, opens: 'In the Land of Green Ginger there is a town called Marmalade, which is inhabited exclusively by guinea-pigs.' In 2017, as part of the City of Culture celebrations, Hull council held a series of events under the gingery heading.

On the Land of Green Ginger street is the George Hotel, the oldest pub in Hull, dating back to 1683. On the wall of the George is a tiny, draughty, vertical slit, believed to be England's smallest window, as explained in an adjacent plaque. It was created in the 18th century to allow publicans to look out for stagecoaches and customers without being spotted. For decades, a porter would wait inside the building, peering through the crack.

Address Hull, HU1 2EA | Getting there The street is 200 yards north of Hull Minster | Hours Accessible 24 hours | Tip A short distance east is the Streetlife Museum of Transport, which showcases vintage cars and horse-drawn carriages (without the horses).

# 43 Philip Larkin in Hull
*Not quite a paragon of virtue*

Philip Larkin is the greatest literary figure associated with Hull. He is commemorated outside Hull's Paragon station with a statue, inspired by the protagonist in Larkin's 1964 work *The Whitsun Weddings* who was 'late getting away'.

Although Larkin was a poet of genius, he brimmed over with bile and vitriol, and that was when he was being nice. Larkin was born in Coventry in 1922. His father was a Nazi sympathiser who attended Nuremberg rallies. The young Larkin arrived in Hull in 1955 as head librarian at the university, staying for 30 years. Within days of arriving he wrote to a friend: 'I'm settling down in Hull all right. Every day I sink a little further.' Four months later, he struck again. 'What a hole, what witless, crapulous people.'

Since his death, Larkin's reputation as a writer has soared. His best-known line is: 'Sexual intercourse began in nineteen sixty-three (Which was rather late for me), between the end of the Chatterley ban and the Beatles' first LP.' Meanwhile, his status as a decent human being has crashed, especially following the publication of his letters. In one he responded to West Indian revelry at a cricket Test Match by claiming that 'a squad of South African police [could have] sorted them out'. Another shocking epigram blasted much of humanity: 'I want to see them starving / The so-called working class / Their weekly wages halving / Their women stewing grass.'

Larkin declined the post of poet laureate when John Betjeman died in 1984, so it went to another Yorkshireman, Ted Hughes. At the 2015 premiere of a BBC documentary about the poet, a woman in the audience condemned Larkin. 'He was a misogynist and racist and he didn't do anything for the image of the city.' Since the statue was unveiled in 2010 his wire glasses have been bent and broken, and one of his arms snapped. Check out the statue before it gets dumped in the Humber.

**Address** Paragon Station, Ferensway, Hull, HU1 3QX; the Larkin Trail can be accessed at www.thelarkintrail.co.uk | **Getting there** Perfect by rail. The station is on Ferensway, the A 165, just north of its junction with the A 63. | **Hours** Accessible 24 hours | **Tip** To honour Philip Larkin's 1955 poem *Toads*, 40 giant toads were placed around the city to mark the 25th anniversary of his death in 2010. Most of the toads were sold for charity but some are still in place, hoping to hop about. One is outside the History Centre and another on Anlaby Road.

# 44 Mother Shipton's Cave

*'The witch's promise is turning, so don't wait up'*

Mother Shipton was Ursula Southeil (c. 1488–1561), soothsayer and prophetess. Like Jumping Jack Flash, she was born during a cross-fire hurricane, but in a cave by the River Nidd, now open to visitors. Ursula was raised in that cave until the Abbott of Beverley took pity and moved her to a proper house. Ursula's mother, Agatha, who was only 15, refused to tell the local magistrate who the father was so her mother was taken to a nunnery and never saw her daughter again.

Ursula became a fortune teller and witch – well, she did wear a pointed hat, had a crooked nose, bent back and twisted legs. Teased by her neighbours, she took refuge in her cave, making potions from flowers and herbs. Such was her renown she features in two of the greatest books of the period. Samuel Pepys mentioned her in his diary from the 1660s, while Daniel Defoe's later *Journal of the Plague Year* (1722) notes 'it became common to have signs and inscriptions set up at doors. "Here lives a fortune-teller", "Here lives an astrologer" … or else the sign of Mother Shipton.' Some came to seek her help for medical problems. Many said she could predict the future: Mary Queen of Scots' tragic execution (1587), the defeat of the Spanish Armada (1588), the Civil War (1640s), the Great Fire of London in 1666, but not, detractors said, that Brian Clough would only last 44 days at Leeds United. Her prophecies were published in a pamphlet in 1641.

Over the years, pedants have questioned the veracity of her pronouncements, but she remains a romantic figure of folklore. She died in 1561, aged 73. Nearby is a petrifying well, the oldest attraction in England to charge entrance, open since 1630. For centuries people believed the water had miraculous healing powers. Anything dropped inside – stuffed birds, hats, boots, toys – instantly becomes 'petrified' because of the calcium deposits in the water.

**Address** Prophecy Lodge, High Bridge, Knaresborough, HG5 8DD, +44 (0)1423 864600, www.mothershipton.co.uk | **Getting there** The cave is located by the junction of the A 59 (Harrogate Road) and the River Nidd | **Hours** Mon – Fri 10am – 4.30pm, Sat & Sun 10am – 5.30pm | **Tip** Head south-east along the River Nidd a mile or so to the Chapel of Our Lady of the Crag, a Marian shrine carved out of the rock dedicated to the Virgin Mary and Jesus Christ dating back to 1408 and easily spotted by the huge figure carved into the outside wall.

# 45__ Town Windows Trail
## *When I'm painting windows*

What a great idea, to fill the many blank Georgian windows in the delightful Dales town of Knaresborough with public works of art illustrating local events and characters. The Knaresborough town windows were just waiting to be filled and have been done so using the technique of trompe l'oeil, which fools the eye into thinking the picture is real.

The surfeit of Knaresborough windows dates back to the days when the Georgian window tax meant that many apertures were blocked up to avoid paying the man. The project to fill in the gaps with this unusual feature was the work of an organisation called Renaissance Knaresborough, set up to promote the town. Some of the inclusions are light-hearted; others historical. There's one for Knaresborough Castle, which was a gift from the 14th-century king, Edward III, to his Belgian wife, Philippa of Hainault. During the English Civil War the castle was briefly held by the Royalists who surrendered after the 1644 Battle of Marston Moor. It was dismantled soon after.

Of the local figures, Blind Jack built hundreds of miles of local roads and is seen playing his favourite fiddle in the pub named after him. The giraffe recalls the town's short-lived late 20th-century zoo. Ginger Lacey was a World War II flying ace whose 18 hits made him more successful than any other pilot during the Battle of Britain. Brian Robinson was the first Briton to finish the Tour de France. Beryl Burton dominated women's cycling in the 1960s, winning nearly a hundred trophies and seven world titles.

Those are the local heroes. But there are famous figures on the trail who have Knaresborough links. Mother Shipton is Britain's best-known prophetess, born locally in 1488. King John strengthened the castle and began the ritual of distributing Maundy money to the poor from there in 1210, while Guy Fawkes grew up in Scotton, just outside Knaresborough.

Address Town Centre, Knaresborough; the Town Windows Trail map can be accessed at www.arttrailproject.org | Hours Accessible 24 hours | Tip Along the River Nidd, opposite the Lido Leisure Park, is St Robert's Cave, home in the 13th century to a hermit, Robert of Knaresborough. Inside is a shelf, possibly fashioned as an altar, while on the platform outside are the foundations of a chapel built to hold Robert's tomb after he died in 1218.

# 46 King Billy Bremner

*Leeds Leeds Leeds!*

Irreplaceable, irrepressible, irresistible, Billy Bremner embodied a thousand years of fiery Scottish aggression in one power-packed ginger-haired midfield football dynamo, taking Leeds United from the middle of the 2nd Division to become kings of Europe from 1964–75.

To call his presence outside the club's Elland Road ground a statue would be to do the great man a disservice. When Bremner made his debut for Leeds in 1960 the idea that he would become a football legend and his team world beaters would have been laughable. Leeds had never won a trophy. Indeed, that year they were relegated from the top division. It all changed when Don Revie became manager in 1961. With Bremner his lieutenant on the pitch the duo transformed the unfashionable, unfancied side. After promotion in 1964, Leeds finished second in 1965 and reached the Cup Final, losing to Liverpool. They went on to win the League twice, the FA Cup, League Cup and the formidable European Inter-Cities Fairs Cup twice. They would have won the biggest prize of all, the European Cup, in 1975, but for the ref.

What could go wrong? When Revie left to manage England in 1974, his replacement was the equally legendary Brian Clough. At his first training session, Clough ranted apoplectically: 'Right you [*deleted*] lot. You may have won all the domestic honours, but the first thing you can do is chuck all your medals, caps, pots and pans into the biggest [*deleted*] dustbin you can find, because you've never won any of them fairly. You've done it all by cheating.' In his first match under Clough, Bremner was sent off for fighting with Kevin Keegan. Nothing was ever the same again.

Frances Segelman's statue was erected in 1999, two years after Bremner's untimely death. In 2006 Bremner was voted Leeds United's greatest player of all time.

1959 – 1976

**Address** Elland Road, Beeston, Leeds, LS11 0ES | **Getting there** The stadium is right next to the junction of the M 621 and the A 643; bus 51, 52 or 55C | **Hours** Accessible 24 hours | **Tip** Stadium tours take place at Leeds' Elland Road stadium, which is a proper football ground, not one of the new 21st-century concrete hell-holes.

# 47__Leeds Refectory Stage
*Another music in a different kitchen*

It might look like a basic university eating area of no particular inter-est, but the Leeds Refectory doubles as one of the country's top live gigging spots. Its greatest contribution to music history is as the venue where rock's greatest live LP, *The Who Live at Leeds*, was recorded on Valentine's Day 1970.

The Who arrived fresh from their triumph at Woodstock, pleased to discover that the Refectory owners had built a new stage so that they wouldn't have to stand on tables. As John Standerline from the university entertainments committee recalled: 'We stacked the amps on dining tables, five each side of the stage, and hoped for the best.' There was nearly disaster: the socials people realised they might not have enough electricity in the system to power the gig and had to call for help from university sparkies.

The Who were then at the peak of their powers: Roger Daltrey at his twirling mic best, Pete Townshend windmilling his arm through power chord after power chord, John Entwistle as sullen and under-stated as ever while crafting a sonic boom of bassness, and Keith Moon tom-tom'ing his way around his drum kit in his customary manic frenzy.

The gig lasted three hours and the band were paid with a thou-sand pound cheque, which they never cashed. Remarkably, Polydor Records released the album in a constrained form. At last, in 2002, the full extended version came out. Musos realised they had been cheated when they discovered that the first track was now the mind-blowing *Heaven and Hell*, inexplicably left off the original, a bit like Beethoven's people forgetting to put *Ode to Joy* on the ninth symphony.

The Refec holds more than 2,000 people. It has witnessed Hendrix, Bob Marley, Led Zeppelin, Floyd and Thin Lizzy. The Who reprised their gig at the Refectory in June 2006 but by then both Entwistle and Moon had transferred to either heaven or hell.

**Address** The Refectory, University of Leeds, Leeds, LS2 9JT, +44 (0)1132 431751, www.leeds.ac.uk | **Getting there** The Refectory is in the middle of the Leeds University campus, just to the west of the A660; it is a 20-minute walk from Leeds city station; bus 1, 6, 7, 9 or 56 from Albion Street | **Hours** Mon–Fri 8am–6.30pm, Sat & Sun 10am–2pm (but reduced hours outside of term time) | **Tip** A few hundred yards north-west of the Refectory is the School of Fine Art where the Mekons, one of the leading Leeds punk bands from the late 1970s, formed after seeing the Anarchy in the UK tour at the Poly with the Clash and the Sex Pistols.

# 48__ Luddite Memorial

*'The workers, united, will never be defeated!'*

Surprisingly, this is the only artwork in the country dedicated to the Luddites, one of the most important groups of political activists in British history. Important, yes, but notorious also, for the Luddites were industrial activists who brought havoc to the new factories of the Industrial Revolution at the end of the 18th century by wrecking the new machines. They even went as far as to burn down the buildings.

Their beef was that every time a new textile machine was developed, new people would be taken on and the traditional workers would lose their jobs. In Yorkshire's West Riding the croppers were badly affected. Their job, to shear woollen cloth smooth, had been well-paid. They lost their livelihoods and found many had been similarly affected across the North. Secret groups formed and called themselves 'Luddites'. The name came from a possibly mythical figure, Ned Ludd, who might have been a young apprentice who broke a stocking frame in Leicester in 1779. In February 1812 Luddites in this part of Yorkshire attacked wagons bringing shearing frames to a mill in Cleckheaton, smashed the machinery, and fled.

The government deemed the Luddites terrorists, sending soldiers to suppress them. There were attractive rewards for information about intended violence. In 1812 Spencer Perceval's Tory government passed the Frame-Breaking Act. This made it a capital offence to take part in extreme Luddite activities. Lord Byron denounced the law in the House of Lords, but 17 men were executed the following year. The troubles died away as employment opportunities grew in Victorian times. The word Luddite has survived to this day as an insult against an individual opposed to getting a mobile phone or maybe central heating.

The statue depicts a cropper brandishing shears, a traditional job threatened by late 18th-century mechanisation, watched by his worried daughter.

**Address** Halifax Road, Liversedge, WF15 8DX | **Getting there** Halifax Road is the A649 and the statue is a mile east of the M62 and Hartshead Moor Services | **Hours** Accessible 24 hours | **Tip** Head to the local Spen Valley Civic Society website, www.spenvalleycivicsociety.org.uk/things-to-do/luddite-trail, for full details of the route that maps out more details about industrial unrest and Luddite activity from 200 years ago.

# 49___Eden Prisoner of War Camp

*No escape for Tom, Dick and Harry*

Don't go looking for any prisoners-of-war. They've all gone. But their camp has been turned into a fascinating museum – Camp Eden – detailing the history of modern warfare, in which visitors can travel back in time for a fully immersive experience.

Eden opened as a prison camp in 1942 when soldiers arrived armed with plentiful rolls of barbed wire and canvas, and began erecting tents that would take enemy prisoners captured by the Allies in North Africa. The first inmates were 250 Italian prisoners who arrived at Malton railway station and were marched through the town to the camp amid the inevitable cat calls and chants of 'Where's your Duce now?' Once in the Garden of Eden, they were forced to build a permanent camp of 45 huts: POW Camp 83.

Eventually Camp Eden housed some 1,200 prisoners as one of hundreds of such camps in the country. Eden was mostly home to Italian POWs, and in 1944 started taking Germans. Inmates spent much of their time farming, and when the war finished, prisoners were allowed to mix with locals who, at a time of strict rationing, were particularly enamoured with the prisoners' delicacy of Italian Prisoner-of-War Mixed Grill: mash, roast potatoes and chips.

The lack of agricultural workers meant the camp remained open until 1948. The camp was then used as a temporary home for immigrants until it fell into disrepair and was used to house farm implements. In 1986, a Stan Johnson bought the site to turn it into a crisp factory, but when three former Italian inmates paid a nostalgic visit the plans changed to a museum. This took shape after discussions with veteran groups and historians. The different huts showcase different experiences. Artefacts ironically include escape plans for how to get out of Germany, although no one ever escaped from Camp Eden.

**Address** Malton, YO17 6RT, +44 (0)1653 697777, www.edencamp.co.uk | **Getting there** The camp is on an unnamed road just north-west of the junction of the A 64 and A 169; train to Malton station, then 2.2 miles by taxi or Coastliner bus | **Hours** Daily 10am – 5pm | **Tip** Five miles south-east of Malton is the deserted mediaeval village of Wharram Percy, the best known of its type in the country. Wharram Percy was occupied for some 600 years before being abandoned c. 1500. It is still possible to trace the outline of lost houses and the ruined church still stands.

# 50_Longest Canal Tunnel
*Longer, deeper, higher*

The Standedge Tunnel is the longest, deepest and highest canal tunnel – all three – in the country. The name Standedge derives from stone-edge, and the tunnel, just over three miles long, forms part of the Huddersfield Narrow Canal, connecting Diggle at the eastern end of Greater Manchester with Marsden in west Yorkshire.

The canal dates back to the period of 'canal mania' at the end of the 18th century when local companies were desperate to connect the Manchester end of Yorkshire with urban areas around Huddersfield by water. The race was on for the first canal to cross the Pennines. Would it be the Rochdale Canal or the Huddersfield Narrow Canal? The Rochdale won, opening in 1804; the Huddersfield not till 1811. By then it had cost £160,000, the most expensive ever then built, constructed by almost 2,000 navvies, nine of whom died during work.

The eastern end of the canal is in Huddersfield, natch. The western end can be found at a watery T-Junction, the Portland Basin, near Ashton-under-Lyne in Greater Manchester. There the Huddersfield meets the Peak Forest and Ashton canals. For the first three decades, the tunnel was used by an average of 40 boats a day, but the tunnel is only wide enough to take one boat. These would be legged through by assistants paid 1s. 6d. for arduous work that took around one hour and twenty minutes for an empty boat and three hours for those with a full load.

By the 1920s canals were passé. The last commercial boat passed through in 1921 and the canal was closed to traffic in 1944. Many locks were partly destroyed and the tunnel became so dangerous it was framed by huge iron gates at each end. However, after a £5 million restoration project it reopened in May 2001. Boaters can now pilot their own boats through using diesel power. Alongside are three railway tunnels whose exhaust shafts appear on the moors above.

**Address** Tunnel End, near Marsden | **Getting there** Just off the A 62 | **Hours** Accessible 24 hours | **Tip** The adjacent visitor centre at Marsden (+44 (0)1484 844298, www.penninewaterways.co.uk), just west of the station, contains displays about the full history of this remarkable waterway.

# 51_ Tunnels to the Centre of the Earth

*It's deep, down, dank, damp and devilishly dark*

Alone and unloved in the middle of Marsden Moor, stands this forlorn brick structure, the Redbrook engine house. Inside can be found two fascinating and frightening wells, covered with steel mesh. The casual interloper might be forgiven for thinking them an opening fit for Professor Otto Lidenbrock out of the pages of Jules Verne, dropping to the very centre of the Earth. More prosaically they're ventilation shafts, leading down an impressive 500 feet to the formidable Standedge tunnels – three for the railway, one for the Huddersfield Narrow Canal – that lie underneath – but they mesmerise and entrance the visitor who can't take their eyes off these openings into the underworld beneath. Remarkable footage of a camera being sent down to take views can be found on Martin Zero's YouTube channel.

This complex was designed between 1798 and 1811 by Benjamin Outram who had just completed the Nottingham Canal. It was equipped with the once revolutionary but by then already-dated early 18th-century technology of a Newcomen steam engine. In a Newcomen, steam is condensed into a cylinder to create a partial vacuum and pressure that can push a piston. A small quantity of water would be discharged into the top of the shaft to induce a strong draught of air that would help the workers down below breathe fresh air.

Outside are 5,600 acres of bleak, brutal, beautiful Marsden Moor, which passed from the Radcliffe family into the hands of the National Trust in 1955 in lieu of death duties. For centuries it had been used as a crossing point from the Manchester conurbation towards Huddersfield. Next to Marsden railway station in the goods yard an old shed has been converted into an exhibition area. Unfortunately, the expanse is regularly affected by moorland fires.

**Address** Marsden, HD7 6NL | **Getting there** The structure is just to the west of the A 62 on a parallel line with Marsden Golf Club. It's a long walk from Marsden station though. | **Hours** Accessible 24 hours | **Tip** There is no alternative but to park the car in a lay-by off the A 62, and walk around the moor, a site of Special Scientific Interest, no less, to do some twitching for grouse, curlew and twite.

# 52 Tees Transporter Bridge

*Bridge of size*

Forget the Angel of the North; this is truly one of the wonders of the North. The Tees Transporter Bridge spans the Tees between Middlesbrough and Port Clarence. It consists of a travelling car – a gondola, if you're feeling Venetian – suspended on long steel cables, which slides along rails on a fixed metallic structure from one side of the river to the other. At no time does anyone think the whole caboodle might drop into the drink. Good.

At 851 feet this is the longest transporter bridge in the world. It crosses the river in 90 seconds carrying up to 200 people and nine cars as part of the A178 Middlesbrough to Hartlepool road. It was always fitting that such a feature would be found in Teesside, a proud symbol of engineering in one of the world's great engineering regions. The idea of a transporter bridge was devised in 1872 by Charles Smith who managed a works in Hartlepool. This one dates back to a 1907 Act of Parliament that allowed a bridge to be built along the Tees only as long it didn't affect river navigation. A compromise was reached; the bridge would move!

The Tees Transporter Bridge opened in October 1911, but the opening ceremony, attended by local dignitaries and Prince Arthur of Connaught (Queen Victoria's grandson), was nearly ruined, as these things usually are, when a bearded man called Arthur Darwin stepped back, unaware that a gap between the bank and the gondola had opened up. He fell off the moving platform and down the opening, severely injuring his bowler hat.

Nowadays the bridge is a major tourist attraction as well as a popular location for extreme sports including abseiling and bungee jumping. After more than 100 years the bridge closed briefly for repairs in 2019 to fix stretched cables and structural defects. There have also been calls for a new bridge, nearer the sea, a more pedestrian bridge, to connect Redcar and Hartlepool.

**Address** Ferry Road, Middlesbrough, TS2 1PL, +44 (0)1642 727265, www.middlesbrough.gov.uk | **Getting there** The bridge is half a mile north of Middlesbrough station by the A 66 | **Hours** All hours. Visitors can now travel to the top of the Transporter in the new glass viewing lift, and visit the viewing area of the Winding House. See website for times of the tours. | **Tip** Head south-east for 10 miles or so to Roseberry Topping, which sounds like the kind of thing you might put on your ice cream but turns out to be the highest point for miles, offering excellent walks and stunning views.

# 53__ Temenos

*A new infant for Gladstone's 'Infant Hercules'*

The smog city's industrial strength as an iron and steel centre has taken a hit in recent decades, despite Margaret Thatcher's famous optimistic walkabout in 1987, but there's always *Temenos* by Anish Kapoor and Cecil Balmond. Anish Kapoor was responsible for the even more bizarre ArcelorMittal *Orbit* by London's Olympic Stadium. This creation, by the River Tees, is supposed to be a gently twisting take on a vast butterfly net and consists of a pole, a circular ring, an oval ring and thousands of yards of steel wire. It was unveiled in 2010 and cost nearly £3 million.

Kapoor and Balmond explained that the structure was on the 'edge of technology', the net alone consisting of 64 points of longitude and 49 different curves. The name Temenos comes from the Greek for a piece of sacred land for worshipping a god. To Kapoor, it compliments and complements the locally worshipped turf of the nearby football club, the perennially unsuccessful Middlesbrough FC, with the net evoking comparisons with the ground's goalmouths. Originally the structure was to be part of the Tees Valley Giants, the biggest art project in the world, with similar artefacts planned for the nearby towns of Stockton on Tees, Hartlepool, Darlington and Redcar. The scheme has been mothballed but Stockton council is hopeful of a revival.

*Temenos* isn't alone, however. An ambitious local cultural project is MIMA, the Middlesbrough Institute of Modern Art, modelled on San Francisco's MoMA. 'There were people who were cautious or had doubts,' explained long-serving Middlesbrough mayor Ray Mallon, 'but a town like ours succeeds when people are proud of it, and our arts programme is an expression of that pride.'

Ironically, just a week before its 2010 unveiling, one of the largest pieces of Teesside engineering was shipped out: a seabed pipe-laying system for South Korea bigger than the Tyne bridge.

**Address** Priestman Road, Middlesbrough, TS3 6RT | **Getting there** The structure is just north of the A 66. Head for the football stadium; train to Middlesbrough station then a 10–15-minute walk; bus to Middlesbrough bus station then a 25-minute walk. | **Hours** Accessible 24 hours | **Tip** Visible from *Temenos* is Middlesbrough FC's Riverside stadium, one of the most obvious examples of the pointless concrete monstrosities that everybody hates, apart from the money men, which in the 21st century have replaced perfectly good, much-loved traditional stadiums.

# 54 Iron Man Display

*Nobody wanted him; now he just stares at trains*

It might be one of the least-used stations in the Calder Valley, with the rail authorities continually running down services that stop there, but the station is a literary treasure trove. The platforms display illuminating boards created by local children featuring *The Iron Man*, the 1968 children's sci-fi novel written by Ted Hughes, the locally born late 20th-century poet laureate.

In *The Iron Man*, a giant metal creature suddenly arrives in England and begins to destroy the countryside, eating farm implements. The opening is magnificent and memorable and tells of how the Iron Man, taller than a house, came to the top of the cliff and answers a series of questions about how far he had walked, where he had come from, and how he was made, each with the answer 'Nobody knows'.

Ted Hughes was born in 1930, a plough's throw from the station at tiny 1 Aspinall Street. When he was seven the family moved to South Yorkshire, but returned to the Calder Valley, to Heptonstall, in the late 1940s. Hughes' lengthy anthology dwells on his Mytholmroyd background where two places caught his imagination: the brooding darkness of the Mount Zion chapel and the looming hill of Scout Rock in the distance. Mount Zion was a building that blocked the Moon 'Darkening the sun of every day / Right to the eleventh hour'. Sadly, it has been demolished. Scout Rock looked like a wall of rock and steep woods half way up the sky. To Hughes, it was his 'spiritual midwife at the time, and my godfather ever since'.

Hughes wasn't just known for his elemental poetry. His private life was a witches' brew of waywardness. He was married to the equally gifted poet Sylvia Plath but in 1962 they separated when she discovered Hughes was having an affair with Assia Wevill, the wife of another poet. A few months later she gassed herself in her Camden Town home. In 1969 Assia Wevill also committed suicide.

# The Iron Man

## Chapter 5

There was no time to be wasted. The Iron Man allowed himself to be taken to pieces, so each part could be flown out to Australia. At the same time a ship sailed from China loaded with great iron girders, and another sailed from Japan loaded with fuel oil. A team of engineers were unloaded on the beach of Northern Australia near the space-bat-angel-dragon's neck. Then the Iron Man's parts were landed and the engineers fitted him together. He stood up on the beach and shouted his challenge.

"Sit up," he roared. "Sit up and take notice, you great space lizard". "I challenge you to a test of strength." The space-bat-angel-dragon couldn't believe his ears. A tiny creature like the Iron Man challenging him to a test of strength? He simply laughed. He peered down out of the sky at this odd little thing on the beach, with the even tinier men scuttling around it. "And if I can prove myself stronger than you are then you must promise to become my slave. And if you don't accept my challenge, then you're a miserable cowardly reptile, not fit to bother with."

The space-bat-angel-dragon was so astounded that he agreed. After all, he could flatten the Iron Man with one eyelash. The engineers had fastened the girders together in the shape of a grid. Under this they had made a steel-lined pit. Now they poured fuel into the pit. They lit the fuel oil and the flames roared up fiercely through the bars of the grid. The Iron Man was stretching himself out on his back, on the grid, among the flames just as if he were in bed. The monster stared down, and the Iron Man smiled up out of the midst of the flames.

The flam[...] Man's ha[...] hot. And [...] hot. And [...] angel-dr[...] Suddenly [...] out. The [...] He coole[...] He went [...] to orange [...] black. N[...] spoke to [...] "If you ca[...] be made [...] me, then [...] and you a[...] The mons[...] laugh. "Al[...] Build the f[...] lie on it." [...] laugh stop[...] Iron Man v[...] upwards, a[...] "There is t[...] you. Go an[...] the sun un[...] red- hot."

Illustrated by: Students of Calder High School School  Sponsored by: A com[...]

**Address** Mytholmroyd Station, Hebden Bridge, HX7 5DT, www.northernrailway.co.uk | **Getting there** The station is visible from the junction of the A646 and the B6138 | **Hours** Accessible 24 hours | **Tip** At the T-junction of the same two roads is the Dusty Miller pub, named after the World War II British prisoner of war who worked on the Burma Railway. The pub includes the Coiners' Restaurant, a rare example of an eating area named after a bunch of popular criminals (see ch. 32).

# 55 __ Tunnellers' Monument
*Train in vain*

Yes, it is supposed to be the opening to a railway tunnel, but at first glance you might be forgiven for asking 'how on Earth are the trains going to get through that?' This six-foot-high Gothic memorial in the churchyard of All Saints, Otley, is a replica of the northern entrance to the gloriously crenellated real Bramhope train tunnel on the Harrogate line nearby. That tunnel, with its arrogant embellishments, was the third-longest in the country when built from 1845–49 and a proud example of the great railway mania of the 1840s when the country was criss-crossed with lines devised by competing companies, in this case the Leeds and Thirsk.

The thousands using the railway every day presumably never gave a thought to the difficulties and dangers in its construction, and so this recreation, created in 1913, honours the 23 miners and navvies killed while it was being built. The railway company found themselves with a most difficult task when they began work in July 1845, on account of valleys and hills, in particular the ridge between Airedale and Wharfedale. What travails took place! Two sighting towers were built and 20 shafts sunk. The navvies came from the Scottish Highlands and deepest Wales, living in shanty towns erected along the course of the line, most known only by their nicknames: Roaring Tommy, Banjo Jack. Indeed, more than 2,300 men and 400 horses were involved in digging nearly 300 feet through just over two miles of solid rock. Any moment there might be flooding, subsidence or, even worse, rock falls.

Commemorated in the Tunnellers' Monument is 22-year-old James Myers whose plaque in Otley church records how he 'died by an accident in the Bramhope Tunnel on the 14th day of April 1848'. On his gravestone in Yeadon it's inscribed: *What dangers do surround / Poor miners everywhere / And they that labour underground / They should be men of prayer.*

**Address** All Saints' Churchyard, Kirkgate, Otley, LS21 3HW, +44 (0)1943, 465927, www.otleyparishchurch.org | **Getting there** The church is just south of the A 659 and 200 yards north of the A 660 | **Hours** Accessible 24 hours | **Tip** Head for the community-run arts centre, Otley Courthouse, based in a former Victorian magistrates' court.

# 56 Mediaeval Wall Paintings

*Once idolatrous, now idolised*

Magnificent mediaeval religious wall paintings can be found in the church of St Peter and St Paul in the delightful market town of Pickering. The paintings, believed to have been commissioned in 1450, show a variety of remarkable religious scenes: the martyrdom of Thomas Becket in 1170, St George and the Dragon, the lives of the saints, the Coronation of the Virgin, the seven corporal acts of mercy, the Passion and the Resurrection of Christ, and the Harrowing of Hell.

The paintings were whitewashed over after the Protestant Reformation of the 1530s, for the new religious leaders cited them as idolatrous. They were rediscovered in 1852 by accident, when plaster fell from the wall. Strangely, the vicar at the time, the Revd Ponsonby, disliked the paintings intensely and described them as 'Popish'. He insisted not only that they be covered up again but that they be whitewashed over. It took the arrival of a new vicar, Revd Lightfoot, in 1876 to remove the whitewash and restore the paintings.

Nikolaus Pevsner, the leading architectural historian, described Pickering's as one of the most complete set of wall paintings in the country, providing 'a vivid idea of what ecclesiastical interiors were really like'. A more recent vicar, the Revd Antony Pritchett, has said: 'I use them when I'm preaching. You can talk about heaven, and you have the whole company of heaven just above your head. Some say the Harrowing of Hell is a doom painting; I say it is a wonderfully positive image of Christ, gripping the wrist of Adam, not letting go, but rescuing all the souls of the damned. The paintings continue to have this amazing relevance. I often just sit in the church and say to myself: I am so lucky to be here. I still see new things in them every single day.'

In recent years, the church has launched an appeal to raise £1.5 million so that they can conserve the paintings.

**Address** Hall Garth, Pickering, YO18 7AW, www.pickeringchurch.com | **Getting there** The church is just north of the junction of the A 169 and A 170 | **Hours** Normal church hours | **Tip** Pickering is the southern terminus of the spectacular North Yorkshire Moors Railway, as featured in the nostalgic and often-repeated TV show *Heartbeat* and the early Harry Potter films.

# 57 __ Castle of Fear

*Perfectly placed former Northern Powerhouse*

Pontefract Castle is now a ruin, and perhaps that's for the best, for it boasts a terrible history of sieges, starvation, civil war and a king's death.

There has been a castle here since before records began. In 1070 it was rebuilt as the 'Key to the North', on account of its strategic site. No expense was spared on the most formidable defences: two outer walled baileys, and 10 internal towers. Pontefract was made for entertaining as well as fighting. The kitchen had four fireplaces, the bakery two ovens, and there were endless bedrooms.

In 1311 the castle passed to the House of Lancaster, so it was really rather unlucky for Thomas, Earl of Lancaster, to find himself beheaded outside the castle walls six days after his defeat at the Battle of Boroughbridge in 1322. A generation later, John of Gaunt, one of the greatest of mediaeval Englishmen, made the castle his main residence.

John of Gaunt was the third son of Edward III, therefore unlikely to become king. But he was the main patron of John Wycliffe, the persecuted religious scholar and England's first Protestant. His speech in Shakespeare's *Richard II* is one of the greatest in canon, a wonderful panegyric to England that contains the lines: 'This royal throne of kings, this scepter'd isle, This earth of majesty, this seat of Mars, This other Eden, demi-paradise'. Ironically John of Gaunt's son, Henry IV, did become king, usurping Richard II who was killed – either hacked or starved to death – at Pontefract Castle in 1400 aged 33.

A century later, Henry VIII's fifth wife, Catherine Howard, committed adultery here with a Sir Thomas Culpeper and was executed without trial. During the 1640s' Civil War the castle was a Royalist stronghold; Oliver Cromwell noted how 'it is situated on rock and therefore difficult to mine'. Once the Royalists had lost the Crown and the king's head, the castle was finally sacked.

**Address** Castle Garth, Pontefract, WF8 1QH, +44 (0)1977 723440, www.pontefractcastle.co.uk | Getting there A 639 then turn left onto Southgate (A 645); five-minutes' walk south of Pontefract Monkhill station; bus 149, 193 or 406 | Hours 1 Apr–30 Sept: grounds Mon–Fri 8.30am–5pm, Sat & Sun 9.30am–5pm; café Wed–Fri 10am–3pm, Sat & Sun 10am–4pm | Tip If you fancy gazing at the stars instead of stone walls, there's the Rosse Observatory on Carleton Road, which hosts regular telescopic sessions (www.gostargazing.co.uk).

# 58 Pontefract Hermitage

*Remarkable survival of an eerie mediaeval chamber*

The remains of a mediaeval hermitage lie below the old entrance to Pontefract General Infirmary. It's a remarkable structure consisting of two chambers carved from the sandstone by mediaeval hermits that sit side by side on slightly different levels, their chisel marks still visible on the walls near alcoves meant for candles.

The Pontefract Hermitage dates from 1386 when Robert de Laythorpe granted the resident hermit, Brother Adam, the site and accompanying land for life. Legend had already surrounded the life of another early hermit, Peter of Pomfret. He was executed by King John in 1213 for predicting the monarch's downfall at the hands of King Philip Augustus of France who had already seized John's lands in Normandy. The story was dramatised in Shakespeare's play *King John*.

Inside the hermitage, a spiral staircase of 63 steps cut from the rock descends from the lower chamber to a pool of water. The upper chamber is known as the Oratory and was founded in 1432 by the 28th canon of Nostell Priory, John de Huddyfield. It measures 14 feet by 8 feet and contains an altar, fireplace, bench and shelf bed topped by a domed ceiling tall enough to stand in. Near the bottom of the staircase is a carving of a skeleton on the wall, possibly belonging to the last hermit before the site was vacated on the Dissolution of the monasteries in the 1530s.

In later centuries, the hermitage became forgotten. It was rediscovered in October 1854 when a workman laying a new sewer fell through the roof. In 1880 Pontefract Dispensary was built over the site, relegating the hermitage to a hidey-hole in the basement. Since the 1970s, the Pontefract and District Archaeological Society has conducted tours of the site, but the building of a new Pontefract hospital nearby disrupted the water table, resulting in the flooding of the Hermitage, requiring continuous pumping.

**Address** Southgate, Pontefract, WF8 1PL, www.pontefractheritage.co.uk | **Getting there** Southgate is the A 645 and the hermitage is half a mile south-west of Pontefract Baghill station; bus 407, 410 or 411 | **Hours** By arrangement | **Tip** The lovely little town museum has a good spread of information about the local liquorice delicacy, Pontefract Cakes, also known as Pomfret Cakes. The two names arise from Pontefract being the anglicised Latin 'pontus fractus', meaning broken bridge, and Pomfret being a corruption of the Norman French version of the same, *pont freit*.

# 59_ Bargate

*Keep out, invading Scots!*

This 20-foot-high mediaeval stone gate is all that remains of a reminder of the area's turbulent past and the extensive walls that once encircled Richmond, the gorgeous small North Yorkshire town. The Normans founded Richmond in 1071 and it soon boasted of the largest corn market in the North. The town grew around the castle, built on the 'riche-mont' or 'splendid-hill', which had four main gated entrances, of which the only survivor is this, Bargate.

Richmond had to be strongly protected early in the 14th century during escalating tensions between England and Scotland. After Edward I's attempts to seize the Scottish throne collapsed when he died just short of the Scottish border in 1307, his son, Edward II, attempted to carry on the fight but was met with huge resistance by the Scottish leader Robert the Bruce. Locals feared that Robert the Bruce would attack south, and so in 1312 Richmond gained permission to surround the outer bailey of the castle with a stone wall to replace the earlier earthen bank. The townsfolk then moved inside the wall to an area now covered by the market square. The threat of Scottish invasion was constant; the walls and gate needed continual attention. After the 1746 Battle of Culloden curtailed Anglo-Scots conflicts, the last of the gates were removed – apart from the Bargate.

Richmond, with its narrow wynds, twisting alleys and steep cobbled market square, is delightful. The name long precedes the London/Surrey version. Henry VII, the first Tudor king, though born in Wales in 1457, was from the family that were the Earls of Richmond. He was so enamoured with the Yorkshire town he renamed Shene Palace to the west of London Richmond Palace, and it became home to Queen Elizabeth. In recent years Richmond has become a well-known Tory stronghold, its MPs including former party leader William Hague and current chancellor Rishi Sunak.

**Address** Cornforth Hill, Richmond, DL10 4QP | **Getting there** Bargate is just north of the River Swale, a short distance west of the castle. | **Hours** Accessible 24 hours | **Tip** The 1080-built castle, constructed to watch over the river crossing, is perhaps the best-preserved Norman castle in the country and can be seen from everywhere in the town.

# 60__Culloden Tower Folly

*No quarter given at these quarters*

This Gothic folly, which looks like the keep of a mediaeval castle, commemorates the last pitched battle on British soil, and one of the most appalling – Culloden.

Culloden was a dark episode in British history. On 16 April, 1746 the Jacobite army of Charles Edward Stuart, popularly known as Bonnie Prince Charlie, was defeated by British government forces led by William Augustus, Duke of Cumberland, on a moor near Inverness. The hostilities would decide who should be on the British throne: the Catholic Scottish Stuart family, who had been unfairly removed from the monarchy in the 1680s, or the Protestant Georgians from Hanover. The last Stuart king, James II, had been persuaded to quit in 1688 for being a Catholic. His daughter Anne, a Protestant, later became queen – in 1702 – but her children kept dying before her. To ensure that the succession passed to a Protestant, the government passed the Act of Succession. When Anne died in 1714 the throne went to the first Protestant in line, George, Elector of Hanover, who was in 52nd position but at least a Protestant. Understandably, the Stuarts staged a number of campaigns to regain what was rightfully theirs, especially when George was succeeded by his son, George II, who couldn't speak a word of English. This culminated in 1746 at Culloden.

Culloden Tower is located in a park to the west of the bustling market town. It was built a year after the battle by Daniel Garrett for the local MP, John Yorke. Garrett was especially talented at Rococo plasterwork, which he deployed in the rooms of the tower. Originally it was called the Cumberland Temple even though the Duke of Cumberland's behaviour after the battle was particularly revolting, writing on a playing card, the nine of diamonds (now known as the 'Curse of Scotland'), an order that his troops should spare 'no quarter' in their bloodshed of the enemy, their own neighbours.

**Address** 1 Cravengate, Richmond, DL10 4RF | **Getting there** The tower can be seen from afar but there are few main roads in Richmond other than the A 6136. | **Hours** Accessible from the outside 24 hours; it is also possible to stay there – visit the Landmark Trust website www.landmarktrust.org.uk for details | **Tip** In the centre of Richmond is a museum dedicated appropriately, given the Culloden Tower, to the Green Howards, the regiment formed in 1688 to support the Protestant usurper, William of Orange. The Green Howards have since been dispersed into other regiments.

# 61 Georgian Theatre Royal
*The playhouse's the thing*

The Georgian Theatre Royal is the oldest working theatre in Britain. It was built in 1788 in what the British Council once described as the 'typical English country town'. The theatre contains all manner of delights: a proscenium with two side doors, a balcony that enables actors to enter either through the scenery or by doors onto the front of the stage, and the oldest set of scenery in the country – that of a woodland scene painted on boards – which dates back to 1818.

The theatre was created by actor-manager Samuel Butler who ran similar establishments in a host of local towns including Beverley, Harrogate and Whitby. Many of the greatest actors of the early 19th century performed here, including Edmund Kean and William Macready. Yet back at the beginning of the 18th century the very act of producing theatre was controversial. In 1700 there were just two venues, both in London, that were allowed to perform spoken drama.

Things began to change as moral restrictions relaxed following the demise of Puritanism. By 1800 there were more than 250 theatres similar to Richmond's with travelling companies bringing the latest plays to audiences far and wide. But there were obstacles. In 1737, Robert Walpole's government passed the Licensing Act, which insisted that all scripts had to be pre-approved by the Lord Chamberlain. He could close down shows in their entirety. On the other hand, audiences would noisily engage in a performance, wildly cheering favourites and heckling villains.

Performances continued here until the 1830s. In 1848 the theatre became an auction house, and later a corn chandler's, furniture store and even a waste paper depot. A trust reopened the theatre in 1968, aptly the year the law changed to cancel the Lord Chamberlain's role as censor. A museum was added in 2002 to display artefacts from the collection and Judi Dench became president.

**Address** Victoria Road, Richmond, DL10 4DW, +44 (0)1748 825252,
www.georgiantheatreroyal.co.uk | Getting there Richmond doesn't lend itself to driving
around, so it's best to park and make for the Friary Gardens and Victoria Road in the
centre of the small but compact town | Hours Mon–Fri 10am–5pm, guided tours on the
hour every hour (booking essential) | Tip Take your time to explore what Lonely Planet
calls 'one of the most beautiful towns in England'. The setting of the parish church of
St Mary is so magnificent an American visitor was heard to exclaim: 'This is what I crossed
the Atlantic to see – an English country garden.'

# 62 Leper Squint of Grinton

*Look closely for an ancient curse*

The Cathedral of the Dales is the name often given to St Andrew's Church in Grinton, Swaledale, where one of its most unusual features can be found on an outside wall. It is a squint window or hagioscope, a Leper's Squint, allowing unfortunates suffering from the dreadful disease to view the service without entering the church.

Leprosy entered England in the fourth century and caused gangrene, even blindness, as well as the loss of fingers and toes. By the Middle Ages it had become *the* epidemic disease, and lepers were not allowed into the building. They were also forced to carry a wooden clapper to warn people of their coming. Many believed it was a punishment for sin while others saw the suffering of lepers akin to the suffering of Christ. Lepers would surely go directly to heaven when they died and were therefore closer to God than most people. The disease retreated following greater immunity in the population; a lesson for our times.

St Andrew's church sits at an important location, a crossing point of the River Swale, the fastest-flowing river in England. The church contains Norman fragments and a chained Bible of 1752, while the porch has grooves in the stonework cut by men who would go hunting as soon as the service ended. The graveyard was the only consecrated ground for miles and was used for burials for the whole territory. Bodies were carried in wicker coffins for 16 miles along the Corpse Way, now known as the Swaledale Corpse Road, resting at intervals on various long stones that can still be spotted. The church's unusual inhabitants are a protected colony of bats.

The village, picturesque Grinton, with its folk music pub populated by muddy dogs, is the first point above Richmond, 10 miles away, that can be forded and the setting for the first bridge upstream of that town. It was included in the Tour de France in the summer of 2014.

**Address** St Andrew's Church, Grinton, DL11 6HW, +44 (0)178 884706, www.swaledalearkengarthdaleparish.org.uk | **Getting there** Grinton is in a very sparsely populated area at the north of North Yorkshire on the B 6270, 10 miles west of Catterick | **Hours** Normal church hours | **Tip** Five miles south is Bolton Castle, a major tourist attraction. Though damaged in the English Civil War, much of it survived and is still in the ownership of the descendants of the Scrope family that built the castle in the 1370s. Mary Queen of Scots was held prisoner here for six months in 1568.

# 63_ Tan Hill Inn
*England's highest pub*

At 1,732 feet the Tan Hill Inn just beats the better-known Cat and Fiddle in Derbyshire as England's highest pub. In fact, the Tan Hill, located between Kirkby Stephen and Bowes, is even more lonely and isolated, 11 miles from the nearest town, its position defying even the most fulsome estate agent.

When the inn was built in 1737 it was known as the Kings Pit, named after a local coal mine, and surrounded by miners' cottages. The only other visitors were drovers leading cattle to the coal pits, although a predictable legend claims highwayman Dick Turpin hid out here in the 18th century. The last mine closed in 1929 and the cottages then started to be demolished. Local farmers kept the pub in business, as do walkers attempting the tricky Pennine Way, which runs nearby.

During the horrific winter of 1962–63 the pub was cut off for 13 weeks and the lemonade froze. In 1974, a huge row brewed when the government messed about with the old county boundaries and attempted to move the Tan Hill Inn into County Durham. In 1987, after much protest, it was returned to historic Yorkshire. That decade the pub appeared in a well-known TV advert in which Ted Moult promoted Everest double-glazed windows by dropping a feather inside. In 1995, the inn became the first in Britain to gain a licence to hold weddings. The most dramatic story connected with the pub occurred on New Year's Eve 2009 when 60 or so revellers found themselves snowed in, unable to leave the pub for three days, which apparently passed in only a few minutes.

The Tan Hill has featured in a number of television programmes including *The Inspector Lindley Mysteries*, *Top Gear*, *The Fast Show*, *All Creatures Great and Small* and *Vera*. Bands such as the Arctic Monkeys have come here to jam. The current owners have discussed installing glass-roofed pods to allow guests to view the Aurora Borealis.

**Address** Long Causeway, Reeth, DL11 6ED, +44 (0)1833 533007, www.tanhillinn.com | **Getting there** The pub is nearly three miles south of the A66, a few miles west of Bowes | **Hours** Normal pub hours. They also have several rooms, including family rooms, and offer facilities to campers and those with motorhomes. | **Tip** It may lie way out east in the middle of the North York Moors, but those looking for historic Yorkshire pubs should check out the 16th-century Lion Inn on remote Blakey Ridge, the highest point for miles. It was here in the early 1970s that the group Back Door revolutionised British jazz, thanks to the remarkable bass playing of Colin Hodgkinson.

# 64__Jane Eyre Inspiration
*Mad manic maid's mansion*

The story of an 18th-century woman confined in the attic of Norton Conyers gave Charlotte Brontë the idea for the bizarre Bertha Mason in her much-loved 1847 novel *Jane Eyre*. Bertha Mason is the mad first Mrs Rochester, locked away in Thornfield Hall, her laughter 'demonic', as she crawls on all fours, 'snarling, and behaving in a bestial manner'.

Norton Conyers is a grand ancient property north of Ripon, first mentioned in the Domesday Book of 1086 when the estate was owned by the Bishop of Durham. It also features Stuart and Georgian additions, Dutch gables and Jacobean embellishments. A late 16th-century owner, Richard Norton, joined the ill-fated Rising of the North, an attempt to force Queen Elizabeth off the throne and replace her with her cousin, Mary Queen of Scots. Norton was duly hanged, his estates seized by the Crown, and granted to the Musgrave family. The name inspired Arthur Conan Doyle when writing one of the greatest of all Sherlock Holmes historical short stories, *The Musgrave Ritual* of 1893.

Richard Graham, the mid-17th-century owner, fought for the Royalists at the Battle of Marston Moor in Yorkshire in 1644. Badly wounded, he fled the 15 miles back to Norton Conyers, pursued by Oliver Cromwell. When Cromwell arrived he found Graham's widow weeping over her husband's corpse, but with a typical lack of sympathy ransacked the whole place. A later bedchamber used by James II and his wife Anne, and their bed, are still on display.

Norton Conyers is open to visitors (but not Bertha's room). Many come to marvel at the romantic walled garden, laid out in 1760 and still used for supplying the house with flowers, fruit and vegetables. Charlotte Brontë explored the place in 1839 and saw the blocked staircase connecting the first floor to the attic, which she mentioned in the novel and which wasn't rediscovered until 2004.

**Address** Ripon, HG4 5EQ, +44 (0)1765 640333, www.nortonconyers.org.uk | **Getting there** Take the A61 north from Ripon and soon turn left onto Hutton Lane. Norton Conyers is about three miles north of Ripon. | **Hours** Garden: Mon–Thu 10am–4pm | **Tip** Four miles south-west of Ripon is the gorgeous Studley Royal Park, which includes the ruins of Fountains Abbey, a Jacobean mansion and a church by William Burges, the greatest of the Victorian eccentric mediaevalists.

# 65 Ripon Cathedral Cartoons
*A maze of moral mediaeval messages*

Samson carrying away the gates of Gaza. A mermaid with mirror and hairbrush. A griffin devouring a human leg. A rabbit disappearing down a rabbit-hole. What on Earth? These are just some of the mind-boggling comical scenes that can be found under the seats of the choir stalls in this magnificent cathedral.

These choir seats are known as misericords – Latin for act of mercy. There are 35 of them, constructed by master carver William Bromflet between 1489 and 1494. The witty moral scenes would remind choristers of their religious duties, although originally such carvings were pagan in nature. The seats were clever; they meant choristers could ease their backs by perching on them while it looked to the congregation that the singers were standing up during such prayers as Matins, Vespers and Compline that were recited with uplifted hands.

Ripon's are not unique. The earliest are from the 13th century and can be found in the choir stalls of Exeter Cathedral. The same workmen who created Ripon's produced similar in Manchester and Beverley. But not only are Ripon's generally regarded as the most interesting in England, they inspired Lewis Carroll's *Alice in Wonderland*. There is even a Cheshire cat featured high up in the South Transept.

Ripon is located where the rivers Laver and Skell meet and was originally known as Inhrypum. It is one of the oldest cities in England and the third smallest. King Alfred granted a charter in 886 and subsequently presented the city with a horn, which is still sounded every night at 9pm, as it has been for 1,100 years.

The Cathedral is formally the Church of St Peter and St Wilfrid, and was founded as a monastery by Scottish monks in the 660s. Saint Wilfrid invited stonemasons, plasterers and glaziers from France and Italy to build the original church as a basilica in 672 and it was then known as Ripon Minster until 1836 when it became part of the first new diocese to be created since the Reformation.

**Address** Liberty Court House, Minster Road, Ripon, HG4 1QT, +44 (0)1765 603462, www.riponcathedral.org.uk | **Getting there** Take the B 6265 to the centre of the city where the cathedral is easily visible | **Hours** Daily 10am–4pm | **Tip** Next to Ripon Cathedral is Old Hall where Lewis Carroll dreamt up the story of Alice in Wonderland in what was the occasional home of the writer's family. Carroll's real name was Charles Lutwidge Dodgson, and for 13 weeks from 1852–58 the Dodgson family would spend time at the hall so that Charles senior could fulfil his duty as resident canon of Ripon Cathedral. While staying here the aspiring writer penned *Ye Carpette Knyghte* and the *Legend of Scotland* for the Bishop of Ripon's children. The property recently went on sale for £750,000.

# 66 Smugglers' Tunnel

*Subterranean setts for seasiders' secret stash*

Just looking at this delightfully dark and enticing tunnel as it enters the sea in the centre of Robin Hood's Bay's beach conjures up images of furtive 18th-century Yorkshire folk entering the chilling chasm to pass contraband bottles of brandy or bales of 'baccy, only to be chased by uniformed flunkeys with three-cornered hats desperately trying to impose the king's laws and taxes on the hapless residents.

The fishing port of Robin Hood's Bay is the most remarkable and romantic seaside village in Britain. Its cottages precariously sidle side by side along narrow cobbled streets by the tortuously steep cliffs. The cellars of the properties are believed to be linked together to aid smuggling, and are filled with a witches' brew of features to aid the infamous industry: tunnels, chimneys, hidden hatches and concealed cupboards.

The shoreline here is pockmarked with rocky coves and caves that made it perfect smuggling territory. Goods would make their way inland on trails running from Robin Hood's Bay to Fylingdales Moor along the Fish Road or Salt Road, often populated by women carrying baskets of seafood or smuggled French lace around their waist to be sold on the black market. Women's dresses with secret pockets made good hiding places. Some even went as far as filling pig bladders with gin to hide under their petticoats.

Of all the smuggled substances, tea was a particular favourite. By the end of the 18th century around 80 per cent of all tea in the UK was drunk illegally, especially when war was directing the authorities' attention elsewhere. Some £10 million worth of revenue was lost due to illegal imports every year although legends abound of customs and village officials taking a cut to keep schtum. Things changed after the Battle of Waterloo with a Navy clamp down and new sea vessels that could no longer land quietly along random points on the coast.

**Address** The Robin Hood's Bay beach, YO22 4SJ | **Getting there** There is only one route into the Robin Hood's Bay: the A 171, with two minor roads leading off. Park at the top and walk down. Don't attempt to drive down and follow in the tyre marks of those who have crashed into pretty cottages *en route*. There is no railway station anymore but coming from the south and west get out at Scarborough and take a bus or taxi along a heavenly route. | **Hours** Accessible 24 hours | **Tip** Robin Hood's Bay is barely spoiled and idyllic. It's easy to spend days exploring all the passages, alleyways, nooks, crannies and havens. Then there is the endlessly fascinating beach with its ancient fossils, occasionally showing up a previously hidden cove. The walks at the top require solid boots and a phlegmatic approach to goats.

# 67 Needle's Eye Folly
*… To go through the eye of a needle …*

Of all the mad follies that can be found in the grounds of the Wentworth Woodhouse mansion, a few miles north of Rotherham, the Needle's Eye comes with one of the weirdest stories.

The structure is a 45-foot-high sandstone pyramid with an ogee arch, topped with a flamboyant urn. It dates back to 1746 when William FitzWilliam, the drunken third earl and MP for Peterborough, took a bet that he could not 'drive a carriage through the eye of a needle'. By the next morning he was sober, but realising the problem he had created for himself, hit upon the perfect, if rather costly, solution. He created an arch wide enough to allow a coach through and called it 'the Needle's Eye'. It later found another good use: for musket firing practice and, some believe, execution by firing squad.

The Needle's Eye is not the only folly here. The 98-foot-high Hoober Stand was built for the Whig aristocrat the Earl of Melton to celebrate victory during the 1745 Jacobite Rebellion. Keppel's Column of 1780 is even higher at 115 feet and commemorates Admiral Augustus Keppel winning his court martial after the 1778 Battle of Ushant. At the Bear Pit, an absurdly over-decorated grotto entrance is guarded by two life-sized statues of Roman soldiers. The biggest beast of all is the Rockingham Mausoleum. This three-tiered Baroque cenotaph is dedicated to Charles Watson-Wentworth, Marquess of Rockingham, one of only seven British prime ministers to have died in office (in 1782).

One feature that hasn't been retained is the original Wentworth Woodhouse garden. On the orders of Manny Shinwell, the highly class-conscious Labour minister, it was bulldozed to be used to extract coal in 1946 and became the largest open cast mine in Britain, right next to the grand house. Given that the coal was of exceedingly poor quality, the decision was seen as little more than an act of vindictive class warfare.

**Address** Coaley Lane, Wentworth, Rotherham, S62 7TF | **Getting there** The follies are visible from the B 6090, near Junction 36 of the M1 and walkable from Elsecar station | **Hours** The Needle's Eye Folly can be viewed 24 hours from the public footpaths; the Hoober Stand and Rockingham Mausoleum are open on Sundays from the Spring Bank Holiday | **Tip** The mansion itself, Wentworth Woodhouse, was a centre of Whig political activity in the 18th century and was Britain's largest private house until it was bought by a trust in 2017.

# 68__ Tea Party Castle

*Boston castle honouring Boston USA & independence*

'The king has said he's going to put a tax on tea / And that's the reason y'all Americans drink coffee.' No epithet better sums up why the United States of America broke away from Britain than those 1976 bicentenary lines from the genius of Alex Harvey about the legendary Boston Tea Party in New England. And no Yorkshire building better commemorates the secession of the colonies from the old empire than this recently restored 18th-century Rotherham hunting lodge overlooking the Don Valley, occasionally glimpsed from the M1.

Boston Castle was a hunting lodge, not a grand castle. It was built by Thomas Howard, Earl of Effingham, within the ancient forest of Canklow Wood and named in honour of the events of 16 December, 1773.

That day, the proto-Americans, who had colonised Massachusetts, threw 342 chests of tea into the harbour at Griffin's Wharf in protest against being taxed while having no say in how their new country was being run. The anomaly was summed up for all time in the famous line: 'no taxation without representation'.

The Earl of Effingham was an officer in the Coldstream Guards and deputy Earl Marshall of England. He was expected to fight for George III against the American rebels. However, he sympathised with the colonists and in the House of Lords criticised the use of British military forces in America. On resigning his commission, he thunderously ordered that no tea, 'that obnoxious beverage', be drunk inside Boston Castle.

The battlemented 'castle' is made from sandstone rubble and only two storeys high. It became disused following the earl's death in 1791 but was later converted into a house, leased out, and later taken over by park keepers. It was refurbished early in the 21st century when the Victorian extension was removed and opened in 2012 as a tourist attraction. The ban on tea remains at pains of a healthy fine.

**Address** 33 Boston Castle Grove, Rotherham, S60 2BA, +44 (0)1709 3366334, www.rotherham.gov.uk | **Getting there** The site is a few hundred yards east of the A630, two miles south of Rotherham | **Hours** 1 Apr–30 Sept Tue, Wed, Sat, Sun & bank holidays 11am–3pm | **Tip** The Chapel of Our Lady of Rotherham Bridge in the minster town itself is one of only six bridge chapels left in England. It has been an almshouse and even a tobacconist's shop but is now back to being a place of worship. The cell doors stand as a reminder of its time as a jail.

# 69__Monolith of Rudston
*True grit*

At 25 feet, this awkward, boat-shaped lump of stone amid the grave-stones in the churchyard of All Saints, Rudston in the East Riding is the tallest of its kind – a megalith – in Britain. It is nearly six feet wide, slender in depth, with two flattish faces and weighs, it is esti-mated, around 40 tonnes. The top looks like a bit of stone has been broken off, which suggests that it was once pointed and would have stood about 28 feet high. In 1773, the stone was capped in lead but that was later removed. The pointed top is now protected with a lead metal cap. Nearby in the churchyard is a smaller version that has been moved away from its parent.

The Monolith of Rudston is made of gritstone. Archaeologists believe that some time around the year 2200 bc it was hauled 40 miles from where they would have found the stone to heave it into place here upright as part of pagan religious rites. Or it might just be a glacial erratic that fetched up there by natural causes. It is likely that as Christianity grew, missionaries fixed a cross to the top.

A wonderful myth says that the devil created the stone when angry that a church was built on pagan lands, and hurled a lump of rock at the heavens, which ricocheted back to Earth. For years a legend grew that a fossilised dinosaur footprint could be found on one side of the stone. English Heritage's geospatial imaging team used terrestrial laser scanning and Structure from Motion photo-grammetry to investigate the surface but were not able to substan-tiate the claim.

The name Rudston comes from the Old English 'Rood-Stane' meaning 'cross-stone'. The Rudstone church here is Norman and was built on what was already a sacred site. The 18th-century antiquarian Sir William Stukeley found many skulls during his dig, which sug-gested that the owners might have been killed as part of a sacrifice. There are many other Neolithic sites nearby.

**Address** Thwing Road, Rudston, YO25 4UY, www.rudston.org.uk | **Getting there** The stone can be seen from the B 1253 in the middle of Rudston, which itself is six miles west of Bridlington. | **Hours** Accessible 24 hours | **Tip** The church of All Saints was begun in Norman times, of which only part of the tower and the font remains. It contains a squint through which the Curate could see when the Host at Communion was elevated. Among the saints on display is an unusual inclusion of William Wilberforce, the local MP who pioneered the abolition of slavery.

# 70__ The House Inside the M 62

*Motorway madness*

It's only an 18th-century farmhouse surrounded by sheep and low moor. There are thousands of them in Yorkshire. What's the problem then at Stott Hall Farm, Rishworth, half way between Littleborough and Huddersfield?

The problem is that on either side of the property roars the M 62, one of Britain's noisiest and most accident-prone motorways, which never stops, night and day, 365¼ days a year. Drivers new to the M 62 gape in amazement when passing and nearly join the great motorway in the sky.

The 1737-built farmhouse stands more than 1,000 feet above sea level and only 40 feet from the westbound carriageway of the M 62. When the motorway was being built in the early 1970s, the owner, one Ken Wild, refused to make way to sell the land his father had bought in 1934. When new owners, the Falkinghams, took over the property they were not impressed to find damp walls, dated décor, and no upstairs bathroom. But they have since transformed it, with a roaring wood burner and proper farmhouse kitchen. There is even treble glazing, but Jill Falkingham has admitted finding the rumbling from passing traffic annoying: 'If you're having a bad day the noise is the last straw. But it's not going away.' Unsurprisingly, vehicles have crashed into the 15-acre plot. At 4.20am one morning a 32-foot lorry ended up overturned in the yard.

The couple work the farm. Paul Falkingham has noted how 'it's got its own climate up here'. And Jill says: 'Working on an upland hill farm is incredibly hard work. The grass doesn't grow because we are so high up and it's so cold. The motorway is the least of our challenges. A lot of people say it's like Wuthering Heights but I think it's beautiful.'

Perhaps there was no stubborn refusal to sell. A geological fault beneath the land meant it was more practical for engineers to leave it be than blast through it. But the former is the better story.

**Address** Stott Hall Farm, Rishworth, HX6 4QY | **Getting there** The house is in the middle of the motorway between junctions 22 and 23, best viewed by a passenger in a vehicle on the M62 and best not to attempt to get there on the side roads | **Hours** Viewable from the outside only | **Tip** This really is one of the loneliest spots on Earth, so head south, back to civilisation, and explore the charming villages of Saddleworth, most of which begin with a 'D' such as Delph, Denshaw, Diggle and Dobcross.

# 71__Moors Murderers Graveyard

*'Dig a shallow grave and I'll lay me down'*

They were the most shocking killings of 20th century Britain, and their legacy still divides those in the North who believe the stories should never be mentioned and those who think their retelling will serve as a warning to the type of people who keep quiet when something appalling happens.

The Moors Murders were carried out from 1963 to 1965 by Ian Brady, a Scot, and Myra Hindley who came from Manchester. They picked children off the streets of the city and killed at least four as well as a 17-year-old boy in the most brutal manner imaginable, usually with a sexual as well as a sadistic motive. They mostly killed in a council house in Hattersley, east Manchester (since demolished) and buried the bodies in shallow graves on bleak, blustery brutal Saddleworth Moor.

Brady's and Hindley's crimes only came to an end when an associate, David Smith, witnessed the final touches of what became their last murder and shopped them to the police. After numerous enquiries, a child they surprisingly hadn't killed took officers to the moors. A search yielded an arm bone protruding from the peat, and it was identified as belonging to 10-year-old Lesley Ann Downey who was still visually identifiable. Police made numerous further trips to the moors – with and without the murderers – to find victims. Brady went to his death in 2017 (Hindley long dead), by which time he was Britain's longest serving prisoner, still not telling officers where they had buried Keith Bennett so that he could have one last hold over the authorities.

Had the pair been caught a few years earlier they would have been hanged, but their incarceration kept the crimes in the public eye. Moors Murders obsessive Morrissey named his group The Smiths after the couple who shopped the murderers to police. Some of The Smiths' mid-1980s' songs deal with the murders.

**Address** The bodies were buried off the A 635, some three miles east of Greenfield | **Hours** Accessible 24 hours | **Tip** Saddleworth Moor is one of the bleakest spots in England and there is nothing to do other than walk and pray for good weather. Ironically, given its fame, there is no actual town or village called Saddleworth. It is the name of one of the largest parishes in the country and comprises a straggle of towns centred around Uppermill, 11 miles east of Manchester, which historically was in the West Riding of Yorkshire and the only section of the latter to be incongruously incorporated into Greater Manchester in 1974.

# 72__ Surfers' Paradise
*Catch the wave*

The Beach Boys sang about how if everybody had an ocean like Califor – naye – ay then everybody would be surfin', surfin' USA. Well, you don't have to go that far to catch a wave. You can do it here on the foamy, frothy Yorkshire coast 15 miles north-west of Whitby. There are surf shops and a surf school. What they can't do anything about is the temperature of the water, but the water babies don't even notice things like that.

But if you don't fancy putting on the waders, digging out the board, and trying to become the next Duke Kahanamoku, then there's plenty to do in this charming seaside spot, too far south to be contaminated by the dying smoggy industries around Redcar. Here the industries have been clean – and mean: fishing and smuggling.

Saltburn is the ideal Victorian resort. The pier was the first to be built on the north-east coast, and is the only remaining pleasure pier in the region. There are Italianate gardens, walks through Riftswood, and the nearby Cleveland Way, which follows a steep path to the site of the Roman signal station at Huntcliffe.

But perhaps the best feature is the classic cliff lift, the oldest funicular in the country. First-time visitors look in bemusement as the car at the top starts to spill water from the back before descending. There's nothing to worry about. The system operates by an amazing feat of hydraulic engineering.

At the top of the 70 per cent slope, the tank fills until it overbalances with the weight of the car 120 feet below. At that moment, the top car starts the journey under its own gravity. Double steel ropes help the procedure. The water is repumped to the top when the car reaches the bottom and the process begins all over again. It's all very easy to understand, as long as you have a degree in civil engineering, and if you don't, it still means the cliff lift is a visually splendid way of traversing the cliff.

**Address** Saltburn Cliff Tramway, Lower Promenade, Saltburn-by-the-Sea, TS12 1HQ, +44 (0)1287 622528 | **Getting there** Take the A 174 to Saltburn Road. Saltburn is some four miles east of Redcar. | **Tip** Five miles east is the Cleveland Ironstone Mining Museum (TS13 4AP), which honours the rapidly declining ironstone mining industry. It is currently closed for a major expansion, so check the website (www.landofiron.org.uk) for details of its reopening.

# 73__Alan Ayckbourn's Theatre

*Amazing person singular*

The Stephen Joseph Theatre is the home of Alan Ayckbourn, Britain's most prolific modern-day playwright, since 1996. Ayckbourn, born 1939, has been responsible for more than 70 much-staged social comedies such as *Absurd Person Singular* (1972) and *Man of the Moment* (1988).

Alan Ayckbourn originally wanted to be an actor. When he told his careers master at his school, Haileybury, the teacher 'slammed the careers book shut and said "Well, my friend, if you want to make a howling ass of yourself, who am I to stop you?"' In 1959 Stephen Joseph told Ayckbourn 'to write plays that would fill the theatre'. He did. For an English playwright, Ayckbourn is second only to Shakespeare in the number of times his works are produced around the world.

Ironically, most of his plays are set in the South. They feature dysfunctional married couples, small-minded bureaucrats, dreadful do-gooders. According to Ayckbourn 'they had to be worthy of my peers and colleagues who were sharing the dressing room with me in Scarborough. They'd come from London and made big cuts in their living standards to do so. If I'd given them tacky seaside stuff they'd say, "Look, I could have been doing telly".'

Ayckbourn was championed by Sir Peter Hall at the National Theatre in the 1980s and was rewarded when *A Small Family Business* took £1 million there in 1987. In the finale, a girl dies of an overdose on a toilet seat while a party rages downstairs, but yes, it was a comedy. Scarborough is proud of Ayckbourn. The feeling in the town is that you can't buy the kind of publicity he brings.

The theatre was originally an Odeon cinema and is designed in-the-round, based on the first such British theatre, which Stephen Joseph himself established in 1955 in the local library. A campaign was needed to find a permanent home, but it wasn't until 1988 when Rank closed the Odeon that this venue was found.

**Address** Westborough, Scarborough, YO11 1JW, +44 (0)1723 370540, www.sjt.uk.com |
**Getting there** By road, the A 64; train to Scarborough station and then a 10-minute walk;
bus 555 or 843 Coastliner | **Hours** Visit the website for production details | **Tip** A mile or so
to the north is the Scarborough Open Air Theatre, Europe's largest open air venue of its kind.

# 74 Anne Brontë Dead Wrong
## *A grave error amended*

Anne Brontë is the Brontë sister not many people read. Like her better-known siblings, Charlotte and Emily, she died at a young age, having written only *Agnes Grey* and *The Tenant of Wildfell Hall*. She is the only member of the famous literary family not buried in Haworth.

Anne Brontë was the youngest of the six Brontë children. She was born into hardship, 20 months old when her mother died in September 1821, and was brought up in a highly religious household. Her father, the Reverend Patrick Brontë (see ch. 29), was an evangelical Church of England minister and the aunt who replaced her mother a Wesleyan Methodist.

Anne came to Scarborough with her sister Charlotte to recover from TB in the ozoney air in May 1849. Journeying to Scarborough for health reasons became popular in Victorian times following the discovery of natural mineral spring waters bubbling out beneath a cliff. The waters tasted bitter, but seemed to cure minor ailments, and so Scarborough became a fashionable spa town.

The Brontë sisters booked a room at No. 2 The Cliff, where the Grand Hotel now stands, a plaque marking the spot. Anne wrote how 'when my foot was on the sands and my face towards the broad, bright bay, no language can describe the effect of the deep, clear azure of the sky and ocean'. Sadly, within a few days she was dead, aged 29. Her death became a posthumous problem. For her headstone in St Mary's churchyard, high above the bay in the shadow of the castle, gave her age as 28. Indeed, Charlotte found five errors on the stone, but the age at which she died wasn't corrected for 164 years.

The Brontë Society has now installed a new plaque. 'Anne was the quietest Brontë and can still sometimes be overlooked in favour of her sisters.' However, she is now seen to be the most radical sister, writing about difficult subjects such as alcoholism and independence.

**Address** St Mary's Burial Ground, Castle Road, Scarborough, YO11 1HY, +44 (0)1723 500541 | **Getting there** The church is easy to find on the spur of land between North Bay and South Bay. | **Hours** Accessible 24 hours | **Tip** St Mary's Church was first built in the 12th century but took a destructive hit during the English Civil War. Internal monuments include one to the late 18th-century travel writer Elizabeth Craven, Princess Berkeley, who also went by the wonderful alternative name of Margravine of Brandenburg-Ansbach.

# 75__Freddie Gilroy and the Belsen Stragglers

*Hero of the concentration camp rescuers*

Freddie Gilroy sits on a bench by the North Sea on the Scarborough coast, wrapped up against the north winds in his overcoat, cloth cap pulled down, a walking stick in his left hand, his right arm draped over the bench. He is a giant steel seated sculpture, but before that Freddie Gilroy was a 23-year-old miner, one of the first soldiers to relieve the Bergen-Belsen concentration camp at the end of World War II. Gilroy and his fellow soldiers found 60,000 emaciated prisoners and piles of unburied corpses.

The sculpture, *Freddie Gilroy and the Belsen Stragglers*, was created by artist Ray Lonsdale to represent ordinary people pulled out of ordinary lives and forced into extraordinary and dangerous situations during war. According to Lonsdale: 'The piece is almost a war memorial, as it depicts the lives of all those who suffered during the world wars. I hope that people get enjoyment from my sculptures but also reflect on the sensitivity and emotion which I have tried to convey through my work.'

Scarborough took a hit in both world wars. On 16 December, 1914 shells hit the castle and the Grand Hotel, where fortunately only two guests were staying. In World War II, German planes attacked the fishing trawlers, and on 18 March, 1941, 98 planes flew over the town, dropping a large number of incendiaries.

After Freddie Gilroy died in 2008, Ray Lonsdale lent the sculpture to the town for a month, but local resident Jakki Willby began a campaign to keep it in Scarborough. Remarkably, Scarborough pensioner, Maureen Robinson, donated the £50,000 needed.

The inscription on the plaque says: *They said for king and country/ We should do as we were bid/They said old soldiers never die/But plenty young ones did.*

**Address** 10 Royal Albert Drive, Scarborough, YO12 7TY | **Getting there** The sculpture can be found on Scarborough's North Bay east of Peasholm Park. | **Hours** Accessible 24 hours | **Tip** A few miles south of Scarbie is the lovely seaside resort of Filey where Freddie's sculptor, Ray Lonsdale, has erected his *High Tide in Short Wellies*, an oversized sculpture of a fisherman on the prom.

# 76 __ Grandest Hotel No Longer

*Candlelight chandelier silver plate crystal clear*

Scarborough's Grand Hotel was cited by Historic Britain in 2017 as one of the top 10 'places, buildings and historical sites that tell the remarkable story of England and its impact on the world'.

This magnificent structure, overlooking South Bay, was the largest hotel and brick building in Europe when it opened in 1867. It was built on the site of where Anne Brontë died in 1849 and designed in the French style by Cuthbert Brodrick, also responsible for Leeds Town Hall, out of local tawny yellow brickwork decorated with beautiful Baroque carvings and sculpted figures. Brodrick deployed the themes of time throughout. The four towers represent the four seasons, 12 floors the months of the year, 52 chimneys the weeks and 365 bedrooms the days, although to be more accurate perhaps there should have been 365¼ bedrooms. The hotel was also shaped in a 'V' in honour of Queen Victoria.

Imagine the shock of the sight of this monumental structure amongst the humble fishermen's cottages, but as soon as it opened wealthy holidaymakers swarmed to the sultry seaside spa town. The hotel bathrooms even incorporated an extra pair of taps so that guests could wash in sea water. Sadly, the hotel was badly bombed in December 1914 at the start of the Great War, and during the next the hotel was made over to RAF trainees. Soldiers came again in 1980, following the Iranian Embassy siege, so that the SAS could train against counter terrorist incidents in huge buildings.

Alas, a decline in its social standing began in the 1970s, which coincided with the flight of millions to overseas resorts. The hotel was bought by Butlins, and later the Britannia group, which caters for the budget end of the market, leading to complaints about all-night noise, inedible breakfasts and the terrible sight of men sat in the lounge on a Saturday afternoon drinking beer wearing just swimming trunks.

**Address** St Nicholas Cliff, Scarborough, YO11 2ET, +44 (0)8712 220047, www.britanniahotels.com | **Getting there** Head to the junction of the A165 and A64 by Scarborough station, down Somerset Terrace then St Nicholas; bus 1, 4, 7, 7A or 8 | **Hours** Usual hotel hours | **Tip** Two of the five local late Victorian cliff railways or funiculars are still in use. The South Cliff one was the first of its kind in the country.

# 77 Jimmy Savile's Missing
### From hero to zero – how's about that then?

For decades he was one of the most popular figures in the country, a flamboyant DJ who apparently invented the discotheque in 1947, and a TV presenter fêted by politicians and royalty. Jimmy Savile was a hero who worked with young people and helped out at hospital wards, performing considerable work for charidee. He was mostly associated with Yorkshire and lived in Roundhay, Leeds, near where he was born. He was knighted in 1990.

Savile died aged 84 in 2011. Hundreds of fans gathered to pay their respects at Leeds Cathedral that November. In Scarborough, people lined the coastal road and broke into applause as the hearse passed by. He was buried in Woodlands Cemetery in the seaside town in a gold-coloured coffin at an angle of 45 degrees facing the coast, 'so that he could see the sea'. He was even laid down in one of his trademark tracksuits as the priest noted how Savile was 'a man who had a place deep in people's hearts'. The headstone was encrypted *It was good while it lasted*, and surrounded by steel bars to obstruct grave robbers.

Then the floodgates opened. Savile was unmasked as a predatory sex offender with a string of atrocities. Indeed, the papers have cited him as the most prolific paedophile of modern Britain. When such claims were made in his lifetime they were ignored, for he had powerful friends. But it all came out in TV documentaries, which led to investigations at the BBC who had employed him for so long and the NHS that allowed him to work at 28 hospitals.

A campaign to have his body exhumed, cremated, and the ashes scattered at a secret location failed to happen when no one would put up the money. Instead the £4,000 headstone was removed and broken up for landfill. Today he lies in an unmarked grave. Other memorials to Savile have already been removed, including an inscription at Leeds Civic Hall and a street sign in Scarborough.

**Address** Woodlands Drive, Scarborough, YO12 6QN | **Getting there** The cemetery lies at the end of a complicated side street system off the A 170 about two miles west of the seaside Spa building. | **Hours** Daily dawn – dusk | **Tip** Head back to the coast to the grand Spa building now used for conferences and concerts. A Victorian cliff tramway links it with South Cliff, 200 feet above South Bay.

# 78__Book Town

*A novel way of branding an old village*

Sedbergh, a tiny place with one narrow main street amidst the hills 11 miles east of Kendal, is now England's official Book Town, the Anglo version of the Welsh Hay-on-Wye. This coup was an ingenious response in reinvigorating the economy following the 2001 foot-and-mouth outbreak that kyboshed the local tourism industry, just as traditional bookshops began to disappear in the internet age.

Sedbergh is now *the* place to find a copy of the official programme for the 1958 opening of the Preston by-pass or the cult classic *Great Railway Eras: Yeovil – 50 Years of Change*. In Avril Whittle's shop a small yellow notebook is made from elephant dung, the ultimate in recycling. As well as the usual books-only shops, volumes can be found in clothes shops, the arts centre and in the various book cafés. One shop is called Sleepy Elephant, a passing reference to Howgill Fells, which was once described by the great walking guru Alfred Wainwright as looking like sleepy elephants. There is even a Book Shelter – an old bus stop where you can take a book for free, as long as you replace it.

The former cinema is now Westwood Books, usually filled with around 70,000 titles, the owners having even moved here from Hay and doubling their turnover. Evelyn Westwood has noted how 'some people worry about going in second-hand bookshops, that they might make fools of themselves if they don't know enough about books'. Some subjects don't move, according to Evelyn Westwood: 'Modern royals, Prince Charles, Prince William, even Diana. Or anything on coronations. They sell newspapers and maybe books first time round, but not second time round.'

Sedbergh's profile rose after being featured in a BBC programme *The Town that Wants a Twin*, which saw it meet up with Zreče in Slovenia. It's so enterprising now there is even an annual Festival of Ideas, covering politics, religion and science.

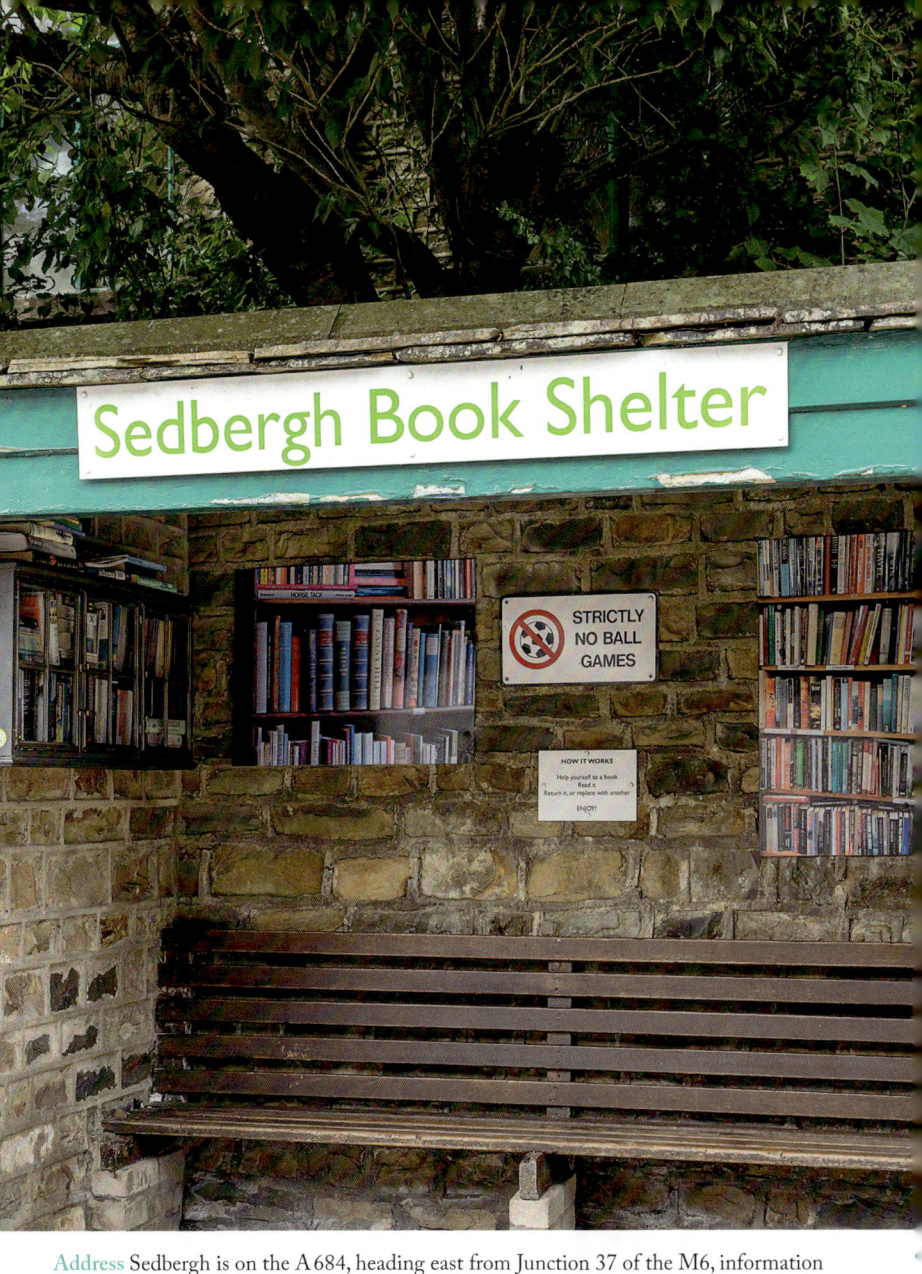

**Address** Sedbergh is on the A 684, heading east from Junction 37 of the M6, information centre: +44 (0)153 920125, www.sedbergh.org.uk | **Getting there** While most visitors come by car, as the M6 is so near, it is far more interesting to arrive by train at Dent. | **Hours** Bookshops are open normal shopping hours | **Tip** There is so much to enjoy in Sedbergh with its twisting little lanes and the Norman Church, St Andrew's, where George Fox, founder of the Quakers, preached in 1652.

# 79___George Fox's Pulpit
*Friends, Yorkshiremen, Countrymen!*

It was by these rocks, on the side of Firbank Fell on 13 June, 1652, that preacher George Fox addressed a crowd of around a thousand people to give birth to the Quaker movement, the Society of Friends.

George Fox was one of many 17th-century religious dissenters whose number had grown once the church authorities allowed people to worship in their own way – as long as they were Protestant! Fox and his followers believed it was possible to have a personal relationship with God, without needing a clergy, and that God existed in every person. His group believed that the established church was corrupt, and so they rejected organised religion, railing against its ceremonies and hierarchy of bishops.

The name Quakers came from a number of references in the King James Bible, especially a passage in the Book of Joel, a minor prophet, which explains how 'the earth shall quake before them; the heavens shall tremble: the sun and the moon shall be dark, and the stars shall withdraw their shining'.

When Fox arrived here that June day in 1652 he was fresh from his famous vision on Pendle Hill where he said he had been commanded to 'sound the day of the Lord' to a great gathering of people. He chose this spot to speak in the chapel, a building that was swept away in the storms of 1840. 'While others were gone to dinner, I went to a brook, got a little water, and then came and sat down on the top of a rock hard by the chapel. In the afternoon, the people gathered about me. There were more than a thousand people to whom I declared God's everlasting truth and Word of life.'

Fox later travelled around England, preaching and teaching. In Derby he told a judge to 'tremble at the word of the Lord'. He even went to the West Indies, hoping to make converts. Fox's Pulpit is an oddly shaped rock next to a disused burial ground. The plaque embedded into the rock tells more of the story.

**Address** The location is on an unclassified road off the A 684 at the Black Horse junction with the B 6256. The site lies about 55 yards along a public footpath. | **Getting there** Firbank Fell lies nearly two miles east of the M6 and a similar distance north of the A 684 about three miles north of Sedbergh | **Hours** Accessible 24 hours | **Tip** In keeping with the wild nature of the locale, head east to the tiny hamlet of Firbank and enjoy glorious walks along the River Lune.

# 80_Kings of Israel Window

*The kings are dead; long live their window*

Selby Abbey doesn't attract the plaudits or tourists of York Minster, but this Norman church is one of the most glorious in Yorkshire. A highlight is the 14th-century east window, which features in gorgeous stained-glass representations of the Kings of Israel.

The dynasty began with David, the second and greatest of all Biblical kings. After the illustrious reign of his successor, Solomon, the Jews' kingdom split into two in the year 930 BC, into Israel and Judah. Unfortunately, of the Kings of Israel, few walked in the ways of the Lord; many supped with the devil.

Zimri was a chariot commander who murdered King Elah but managed only seven days in the hot seat – a bit Lady Jane Grey-ish. Ahab was a wicked king in thrall to his horrific wife, Jezebel. They ejected the Jewish God and brought in worship of the infidel Baal. Ahab's name has remained in the public eye after being used for that of the vengeful captain in *Moby Dick*. Jehu ordered his men to kill all the royal princes, which saw 70 heads left outside the city gate. At least under Jeroboam II ancient Israel prospered, trading in olive oil and wine. The Israel line stopped with Hoshea but according to the New Testament, the kings on the other side, the House of Judah, went all the way down through the generations to Jesus himself.

Selby Abbey became one of the wealthiest monasteries in Yorkshire but fell during the Dissolution. The buildings alongside have long since withered away, leaving only the church. Also inside, in the south clerestory of the choir, is the 15th-century Washington Window. Look out for three red stars above two red bands on a shield, the earliest depiction of the arms of the Washington family. It was this heraldry, thought to commemorate John Wessington, the 15th-century Prior of Durham, an ancestor of George Washington, that inspired the American flag of stars and stripes.

**Address** Selby Abbey, The Crescent, Selby, YO8 4PU, +44 (0)1757 703123, www.selbyabbey.org.uk | **Getting there** The abbey is near the River Ouse on the A 19; train to Selby station and a 10-minute walk across Selby Park | **Hours** Daily 10am–4pm, although visiting may be restricted during service times | **Tip** For a spectacular secular experience, head five miles south-east to the phenomenal cooling towers of the Drax power station, Britain's largest, built in 1973 as the last major coal-fired power station to go up in the UK.

# 81 Cholera Monument

*Testament to a pandemic killer of the past*

In a hundred years time there will be memorials to those who died of coronavirus, 2020–21, but this monument is a fitting tribute to one of the great killers of the early industrial era – cholera.

In 1831, the people of Sheffield were pondering over whether the Blue Death, as it was called, was likely to come to the city. On 1 July the *Sheffield Courant* reassured everyone by explaining that 'alarm is entirely groundless'. Nevertheless, the dreadful disease did arrive, having travelled from Russia across Europe. Some were more susceptible than others. 'It attacks chiefly the dirty, the idle, the drunken, and the disorderly', the *Sheffield Mercury* explained. On 16 December the *Courant* was advising locals that 'the Overseers of the Poor of Sheffield respectfully call upon the inhabitants to cleanse their houses, yards, and premises'. Such a warning compares with the March 2020 call by the UK government for people to wash their hands to eradicate coronavirus.

Cholera claimed 50,000 lives in Britain, 402 of them in Sheffield out of the 1,300 who caught the disease. The local dispensary issued more than 3,500 leeches that year; normally it was around 100. Nearly 20 years later there was another national outbreak when 33,000 died, although there were only 100 fatalities in Sheffield. What no one knew at that stage was that the chief cause was dirty, foetid water and that the best cure was clean water, of which there was increasingly less in an increasingly dirty society. The mysteries around cholera were solved by a London doctor, John Snow, in the 1850s.

This Gothic memorial is dedicated to the 402 who died in 1832 and are buried here in the grounds between Park Hill and Norfolk Park adjoining Clay Wood. It was designed by Matthew Hadfield who was also responsible for Sheffield Cathedral. The memorial was struck by lightning in 1990 and the top was removed.

Address Norfolk Road, S2 2SX | Getting there Visible from junction of A61 and A6135, 400 yards south-east of Sheffield station | Hours Accessible 24 hours | Tip A mile east is the equally historic Manor Lodge or Manor Castle from 1516, the country retreat for George Talbot, the 4th Earl of Shrewsbury, where Mary Queen of Scots was held prisoner by the 6th earl in the 1570s.

# 82 The Hubs

*Museum: Don't you want me? Public: No!*

Fifteen million pounds is a lot to spend on a students' union for Sheffield Hallam University, but this is no ordinary students' union. The Hubs was the short-lived National Centre for Popular Music, a farcical millennial project. It opened in March 1999 and was gone by July 2000, having been shunned by the public. The anticipated 400,000 visitors a year never materialised. But then tickets were £21 for a family of four. The closing night appropriately featured Madness.

The centre was meant to symbolise the regeneration of post-industrial Sheffield, but music people asked why this location was chosen and not the more obvious Manchester or Liverpool. Well, Sheffield does have a proud musical heritage. Joe Cocker was a gas fitter who became a phenomenal songwriter (Sandpaper Cadillac) and the world's greatest interpreter of other people's songs at the end of the 1960s (apart from Rod) before going soft in the 1970s. Jarvis Cocker (no relation) preened and pouted his way around the overrated Britpop explosion of the 1990s. In between, in the 1980s, the Human League and their Heaven 17 spin-off pioneered synth pop. Indeed, the main part of the museum featured Soundscapes, a 3D-surround sound auditorium with an ambient soundtrack written by Heaven 17's Martyn Ware.

Yet, bizarrely, the museum mostly ignored Sheffield's greatest music creation, the remarkable, ground-breaking electro pioneers Cabaret Voltaire, arguably the most influential British group since the Beatles, who made their mesmerising masterpieces at the nearby Western Works, since sadly demolished. Presumably they were too outré for the museum's management; their omission a bit like leaving Mozart out of a music museum in Salzburg.

Branson Coates' four giant stainless steel drums, each featuring a rotating turret with a nozzle designed to turn with the wind and vent air, have remained.

**Address** 6 Paternoster Row, Sheffield, S1 2QQ, +44 (0)114 225411, www.hallamstudentsunion.com | Getting there The Hubs is a few hundred yards west of Sheffield train station near where the A 61 splits into three parts | Hours Normal working hours and for evening events, check the website for details | Tip Just to the north is a more successful millennial project – the Millennium Gallery. It opened in April 2001 and is worth visiting for its collection of watercolours, drawings, prints, plaster casts, minerals, illustrated books, coins and manuscripts that belonged to John Ruskin, the key inspiration on art, architecture and design in Victorian Britain.

# 83_ Sex Scandal Church
*Church of the poisoned mind*

Not many churches find themselves associated with the kind of salacious history that disfigured St Thomas, Crookes in the 1990s. The church hit the headlines due to the outré nature of its Nine O'Clock Service that mixed rave music with sexual braggadocio and saw the vicar, Chris Brain, sacked for sexually abusing female members of his congregation.

In 1992, the Revd Brain announced his intention of exploring human sexuality. 'You don't have to enter the service and leave your bollocks outside', he tastefully announced. The tabloids pounced and dubbed him the 'rave' vicar whose ecclesiastical offerings proposed a corporeal as well as a spiritual service. There were overhead projections, pounding music and Brain himself in Messianic robes. Men in T-shirts and girls in mini-skirts created an ambience that was part-cathedral, part-nightclub to a congregation where the average age was 24, a few decades short of that usually found among church worshippers. Beyond the dancing and bacchanalia there was more discussion about the future of the planet than of anything as outdated as the role of God. Communion was fun. Brain would rub his chest with soil in the sign of the cross. The wafer consisted of hamburgers. At least the blood of Christ was wine, rather than Rolling Stones-style Jack Daniels.

In 1995, complaints appeared about the sexual abuse of women in the congregation. The Diocese led an inquiry and shut it all down. Brain confessed to having enjoyed what the Bible would call 'carnal knowledge' with young women in his flock. There were calls for him to be defrocked, and he resigned in November 1995, a week before a TV programme captured the whole bizarre business, booking himself into a psychiatric hospital. The church banned Brain from practising and he left for America to make it as a rock musician. The church is now STC Sheffield, an ecumenical establishment.

**Address** Nairn Street, Sheffield, S10 1UL, +44 (0)1142 671090, www.stthomascrookes.org |
**Getting there** The church is located about a half-mile north of the A 57 (Manchester
Road) in the suburb of Crookes and a mile west of Sheffield train station | **Hours** Normal
church hours | **Tip** Sheffield is clearly the city for unusual church experiences. The Church
Temple of Fun is a bar with a vegan restaurant, the décor inspired by South American
religious iconography, featuring retro arcade games and that now rarity, a pool table. The
commandments include 'Sanitise Thy Hands' and 'Thou Shalt Not Pay With Cash'.

# 84__Freddie Trueman in Flight

*Fearless in full flow*

Two recent cricketers sum up the glories of the legendary Yorkshire County Cricket Club: Geoff Boycott (batsman) and Freddie Trueman (bowler). Trueman was described by 1960s' prime minister Harold Wilson as the 'greatest living Yorkshireman', though not as great as Wilson himself of course, but he was one of the greatest ever fast bowlers, the first to take 300 wickets in a Test career. He was also an excellent fielder at leg slip and handy with the bat in the late order, making three first-class centuries – unusual for a bowler.

Trueman was known as 'Fiery Fred' and played for England 67 times but was often omitted for clashing with the cricket establishment whom he criticised for snobbishness and hypocrisy. Nevertheless, for England's 1000th Test in August 2018 he was named in the country's greatest Test XI. On retiring he became a popular author and a witty broadcaster. 'There's only one head bigger than Tony Greig's, and that's Birkenhead', he joshed about the former England captain.

Shortly before his death from cancer in 2006, Trueman discovered that his grandmother was Jewish, which meant that his mother was Jewish and that he was Jewish, even though his own mother had not acknowledged this. It gave him a rare double status: of being a Jewish cricket professional and of being a Jew called Fred. He said he was happy to be considered Jewish but joked that it was too late to give up on the bacon sandwiches.

The statue rests by the Leeds–Liverpool Canal in Skipton, which Trueman made his home town and where he died in 2006. It cost £90,000 and was the work of Graham Ibbeson who has also done Eric Morecambe, Benny Hill and the umpire Dickie Bird in Barnsley. It captures the form and fluency of his bowling. Trueman's widow Veronica explained how 'You can feel him releasing the ball, and there's that slight grin on his face as he knows he's got a wicket.'

**Address** Off Bridge Street by the Leeds–Liverpool Canal, Skipton, BD23 1LH | **Getting there** The A 6131 crosses the canal just south of the statue | **Hours** Accessible 24 hours | **Tip** Skipton as a place to visit is delightful. The town is the gateway to the Dales. There's a well-preserved 900-year-old castle, a market best seen on Sheep Day, with sheep dog trials and sheep shearing, and the length and breadth of the canal to perambulate along.

# 85 Anti-Virus Tomb
*Could tomb of Edwardian aristo solve pandemics?*

Sir Mark Sykes' politics may have caused more turmoil than those of most 20th-century politicians, but his remains may yet help scientists in their fight against mutating viruses. In 2008, during the brief panic about bird flu, his tomb was opened to discover how he died in the flu epidemic of 1918 – 19, nowadays described popularly as 'Spanish Flu'.

Sir Tatton Benvenuto Mark Sykes was a diplomat, adventurer, and MP for Hull Central. He was the British government's lead negotiator in devising the modern map of the Middle East. In 1916 he secretly carved up a deal with France to divide the Ottoman Empire. Everything north of an imaginary line in the sand would come under French influence, thereby creating modern-day Syria and Lebanon, while everything south of the line would be British, resulting in modern-day Israel and Jordan. And they all lived happily ever after.

In 1919, Sykes became one of the estimated 50 million victims of the raging flu, aged just 39. It was only by the good fortune of his having been buried in a lead-lined coffin, which slows the decay of soft issue, that it could be opened to be examined in 2008, but it took two years to gain permission from all his descendants and the Diocese of York to carry out the exhumation. The coffin was opened at a service here in the rural Yorkshire churchyard where he is buried. Unfortunately, it had split owing to the weight of the earth on top, the corpse badly decomposed. Frozen in liquid nitrogen, it was taken to a laboratory for researching defences against future pandemics, something that few took seriously until the fateful year 2020.

Interestingly, back in 2007 – 08, during the bird flu worries, experts warned that the next one was overdue. Sir Liam Donaldson, the government's chief medical officer, said: It will come, it will be real, and only if we plan can we reduce its impact.'

**Address** St Mary's Churchyard Sledmere, East Riding, YO25 3XG | **Getting there** Off the B 1251, seven miles north-west of Driffield | **Hours** Accessible 24 hours | **Tip** The Sykes family commissioned a tall stone replica of the Eleanor Cross for the centre of the village. The Eleanor Crosses were a series of 12 monuments erected across England from Lincoln to Charing Cross by Edward I while mourning the death of his wife, Eleanor of Castile in 1290. Only those at Geddington and Hardingstone in Northamptonshire, and Waltham Cross, just north-east of London, survive.

# 86 _ Canal Lock from Hell

*'Drag my canal, you saucy old salt'*

The Tuel Lane lock near the Yorkshire terminus of the Rochdale Canal in Sowerby Bridge is the deepest in the country. It features a jaw-dropping fall of almost 20 feet and can only be operated by the lock-keeper, not boat crews. It replaced two previous locks, Nos. 3 and 4, near the canal's junction with the Calder and Hebble Navigation.

The Rochdale Canal is the most heavily locked in the country. It had to be, given the contours of the Pennines between West Yorkshire and Manchester, and so 36 locks descend from the summit near Littleborough to Sowerby Bridge. The canal came into being after a meeting in 1776 of 48 Rochdale men who raised more than £200 and hired the great James Brindley, the engineer who had created the first ever industrial canal, the Bridgewater, in 1761. But it took decades for the canal to be completed. It wasn't until 1804 that it was ready. However, connection with other waterways in Yorkshire and Lancashire meant that for the first time canal vessels could get from the Irish Sea to the North Sea right through the middle of the country.

The Rochdale Canal became a vital transport medium for the industry that sprung up in the local Calder Valley – water-powered cotton and worsted spinning mills and woollen scribbling mills in the early days of the machine age. It transported cotton, wool, coal, limestone and salt despite stiff competition from the nearby railway from the 1850s. Decline set in after the Great War. The canal closed to traffic in the 1930s and was officially abandoned by an Act of Parliament in 1952. In Sowerby Bridge part of the route was filled in for a road. Fortunately, opposition from the Inland Waterways Association led to the founding of the Rochdale Canal Society in 1974, followed by restoration, even where bits of motorway had cut through. The lock was restored from two old locks and reopened in 1996.

**Address** Junction of Rochdale Canal and the A 6139 | **Hours** Accessible 24 hours | **Tip** The perfect way of exploring the canal system is with Brontë Boats. Although this is not exactly Brontë country, Branwell Brontë, the black sheep of the famous family, did work as a clerk at Sowerby Bridge railway station.

# 87 — War of the Roses Memorial
*Yorkshire's cross to bear*

This memorial in Towton, near Tadcaster, marks the local War of the Roses battle on 29 March, 1461, Palm Sunday. It was one of the most ferocious and bloodiest in English history. Two of the largest armies ever assembled, possibly as many as 100,000, saw the Yorkists in a blizzard winning a decisive victory over the Lancastrians on this hill just east of Leeds.

Towton was a good site for a war. It was undulating land with a high point and it was the Lancastrians who chose it. There was a fast-flowing stream and trees to stop any large group from approaching in formation. The Lancastrians were loyal to Henry VI. The Yorkists claimed their problem was not so much the king but his useless and corrupt advisers, and Henry was too weak to stop tension mounting. Over at the Battle of Wakefield, leading up to Towton, Richard, 3rd Duke of York, was killed, his head then displayed on a pole at York's Micklegate. Two of his sons, however, became kings of England – Edward IV and Richard III – but his demise led to the Battle of Towton.

On reaching Towton, Edward's army was equipped with cannon and handguns. Yet not all the Yorkist army was even at the site when fighting began, and more than 28,000 men lost their lives. Following the battle, people crossing Cock Beck trying to keep dry had to stand on the bodies of drowned Lancastrians. Lord Dacre, a Lancastrian, got a better deal. He is buried in Saxton churchyard standing upright alongside his horse. Skeletons of Lancastrians found beneath the floor at nearby Towton Hall have scratch marks on the sides of the skulls, caused by having had their ears cut off as trophies. After the battle, Edward IV replaced Henry VI on the throne to establish the House of York.

This ancient cross is one of only 50 of its type left in the country, as many were slashed during the iconoclasms of the Cromwellian period.

**Address** B 1217, Towton, near Tadcaster, LS24 9BF | **Getting there** The memorial is on the B 1217, a mile south of its junction with the A 162. Towton is a couple of miles east of the junction of the A 1(M) and the A 64 | **Hours** Accessible 24 hours | **Tip** Tadcaster itself is best known as being the home of Yorkshire's finest ales, those brewed by Sam Smith's, in the news in recent years after the owner, Humphrey Smith, shut one of his pubs when he overheard a man swearing while he was visiting. Other Sam Smith's have banned mobile phones and tablets.

# 88__White Horse of Kilburn

*It ain't no desert, and the horse has a name*

It's a huge blanched stallion cut into the hillside in the North York moors near Roulston Scar, 318 feet long, 220 feet the other way, covering nearly two acres as the largest hill figure in England.

The White Horse of Kilburn is visible from the East Coast railway line south of Thirsk. On a clear day it can be seen from Leeds, while in recent years its fame has grown due to exposure by aerial cameras during cycle races. The horse was created in November 1857 when 33 men took the topsoil off to expose the rock underneath and then covered it with limestone chips whitened and sealed with six tons of lime. It was the work of school master John Hodgson and his pupils, influenced by a Thomas Taylor who was a buyer for a London firm and attended the celebrations at Uffington White Horse in Berkshire in 1857.

Yet to some chevalier purists, the horse is a fake, as it was carved into a steep grey limestone hill rather than a traditional chalk hill, and it's been nicknamed the 'Old Grey Mare' because of its true colour. From the top of the hill one can enjoy what author James Herriot called 'the finest view in England'.

There are 16 or 17 such horses, depending on which ones are counted. Most are ancient. For instance, the one in Westbury, Wiltshire, was cut to commemorate King Alfred's victory at the Battle of Ethandun in 878. The Osmington White Horse of Dorset shows George III riding his steed. However, that of Devizes, Wiltshire, was created for the 2000 Millennium celebrations.

During World War II the horse was covered up to befuddle enemy bombers looking for the landmark. Much work has been needed and undertaken by volunteers to groom the beast, given the steep gradient of the hillside. Now the fear is, if more lime chips are added to maintain the whiteness, the weight will see it slip down the hill. A dash of paint is regularly added by the Forestry Commission.

**Address** Low Town Bank Road, Kilburn, near Thirsk, YO61 4AN | **Getting there** From Thirsk, take the A170 to Hambleton and head south | **Hours** Accessible 24 hours | **Tip** Leave the horse and head to Thirsk for the Birds of Prey Centre to see these magnificent flyers – eagles, falcons, hawks, kites, vultures and owls – up close and marvel at how they don't fly away.

# 89 Gaddings Dam

*Britain's highest beach*

It might be nearly 50 miles to the nearest seaside at Lytham, but Todmorden, which straddles the Lancs–Yorks border 17 miles from Manchester, boasts the country's highest altitude beach at Gaddings Dam, run by volunteers who rescued it from closure in 2001.

At 300 yards above sea level, Gaddings is highly exposed and one of the windiest beaches in the country, with no shelter from the sun the one day Sol comes out to play. Swimming is safe, as long as you keep to the walls to avoid the nasty rocks. The water is clean, and obviously there are no tides or currents, but nor are there lifeguards or in fact any facilities at all. Another downside is the steep trek up the hill on a muddy and slippery footpath to get there.

This one is the western dam; the eastern dam is now empty. They were built by the Rochdale Canal Company in the early 19th century to supply water to the valley below using convict labour from the Salford House of Correction. Indeed, nearby is one Jail Hole Quarry. Surrounding the dam is Langfield Common, moorland above the hamlets of Lumbutts and Mankinholes whose history dates back to the Reformation, when the owner, Sir Stephen Hamerton, rebelled against Henry VIII, and was hanged and beheaded for his sins in 1537.

In World War II the dam was drained to prevent the Germans using it as a navigation aid at night when the Moon might reflect from its surface. It was also used for Territorial Army training. By the 1960s the valve mechanism was faulty and the reservoir was emptied. It took two years to refill in the 1960s. A complex of sluice gates can still be traced on the moor land around the dams.

Because of regular changes of governance no one is certain whether Todmorden is in Yorkshire or Lancashire. The ancient boundary – the River Calder – runs through the market town. In recent years Tod has become bizarrely associated with claims of UFOs; there are even UFO meetings in local pubs (see ch. 92).

**Address** Off Lumbutts Road, Todmorden, OL14 6JJ | **Getting there** Take the A 6033 towards Walsden station. The dam can be reached via a path opposite the Shepherd's Rest Inn, but visitors are asked not to park in the pub car park; train to Todmorden station; bus T 6 or T 8 from Todmorden bus station to the Shepherd's Rest. | **Hours** Accessible 24 hours | **Tip** Head north to Todmorden itself and a few miles beyond for a great hike to the weird rock formations of the Bride Stones and Wizard of Whirlaw.

# 90__ Stoodley Pike

*A monument to peace atop a bleak moor*

Stoodley Pike Monument dominates the bleak landscape just south of the route from Hebden Bridge to Todmorden at the western end of West Yorkshire, phallicly pointing to the sky enticing curious onlookers.

The tower stands 121 feet high and rests on a sturdy plinth atop the 1,300-foot hill itself known as Stoodley Pike. The site contains a Bronze Age burial cairn which, according to local legend, if removed could lead to strange lights playing around the hill, a scenario that could excite the makers of *Quatermass* into a new series, surely. It was designed in 1854 by local architect James Green and completed two years later at the end of the Crimean War.

This tower replaced an earlier monument that had been created to commemorate the restoration of peace throughout Europe after victory over Napoleon at the Battle of Leipzig in 1814. The only problem was that peace didn't last long once Napoleon had escaped from Elba. Work on the monument then restarted when Wellington vanquished Napoleon at Waterloo in 1815. At least it stood there for almost 50 years, collapsing on 8 February, 1854 after a lightning strike on the day the Russian ambassador left London just before the declaration of war with his country.

Stoodley Pike is so remote it can't be reached by car and is accessed best by walkers from the nearby Pennine Way. The monument contains a spiral staircase of 39 steps that can be accessed from its north side. There are no windows, just a small grille that lets in a bit of light, so visitors are advised to bring a torch. It's well worth the effort of climbing to the top as there are fantastic views from the viewing balcony. A Star of David on the structure denotes the Masonic influence from those who commissioned it. In 2014, to mark the monument's bicentenary, a festival was held, with a samba group and a brass band. Two hundred homing pigeons were released.

**Address** Stoodley Pike, Todmorden, OL14 6HB | **Getting there** The monument is in the countryside on the Pennine Way, not on any road, a mile south of Eastwood off the A646 | **Hours** Accessible 24 hours | **Tip** Take the opportunity to explore along the Pennine Way, often described as the backbone of Britain, stretching from the Peak District to the Scottish Borders.

# 91__The Summit

*Summat's oop*

It's the top, the summit, the toppermost of the toppermost, the highest spot for miles, some say in the whole of Yorkshire, and in olden times they said of the world. And it announces itself with a nasty looking peak whose mouth contains the dramatic opening of a railway tunnel cut at the very south-western tip of Yorkshire.

The story is not of the peak but of the tunnel, the legendary Summit railway tunnel, one of the world's oldest. It was the longest, at just over a mile-and-a-half, when it opened on the Manchester–Leeds railway on 1 March, 1841. Brute strength and hand tools completed the work, the only illumination candlelight, the spoil used to create Blackpool prom. The cost shot up, HS 2 style, to £251,000. Given the lax health and safety rules of the day, it was no surprise that 41 workers died. But it meant that there was now a quick means of crossing from Lancashire into Yorkshire and vice versa.

The tunnel was designed by Thomas Gooch who used 23 million bricks and 8,000 tons of mortar. But it was Gooch's assistant, Barnard Dickinson, who uttered the most memorable claim: 'This tunnel will defy the rage of tempest, fire, war or wasting age.' That proved correct when, despite a huge fire in December 1984 that saw flames rising high over the hillsides, the Summit Tunnel re-emerged, ready to resume its purpose. The reopening was celebrated by the one-off opportunity of a mass walk through organised by Todmorden Rotary Club.

The railway line here is the slow, wildly picturesque route connecting Manchester Victoria and Leeds, which contrasts with the sharp speeds on the Manchester Piccadilly to Leeds line further south. Not that that has stopped southern-based politicians from regularly promising an unnecessary third line between the two cities every time there are moans about HS 2, obviously unaware of the amount of tunnel boring that work would entail.

**Address** Todmorden Road, Calderbrook, OL15 9QX | **Getting there** Off the A 6033, between Walsden and Littleborough | **Hours** Accessible 24 hours | **Tip** Appropriately enough for an area defined by its summitness, there is a hamlet on the road north to Walsden called Bottoms, with a Bottoms Farm, Bottoms Mill and an amply stocked Bottoms Mill Shop.

# 92__The UFO Pub

*It's pub life, Jim, but not as we know it*

Todmorden, the small town so enmeshed at the historic border of Lancashire and Yorkshire no one can remember which county it is in, is also the UFO capital of England. And if anyone wants to discover more, they should head to the regular meetings at this pub.

The Golden Lion was run down until the Walkers took it over in 2015. They put on art classes and gigs by major acts including Jarvis Cocker, and hit the headlines in 2014 when a bid to paint the exterior bright canary yellow in anticipation of the arrival of the Tour de France saw them threatened with a £20,000 fine. In 2020, the pub became a community hub during the coronavirus pandemic.

But why the local interest in extra-terrestrial life, with hundreds heading for the Pennine hills around the town to look for sightings? It all began not at Broken Bow, Oklahoma, but at Leeds when 56-year-old miner, Zigmund Adamski, left his house one day in June 1980 to go shopping and was never again seen alive. Five days later his body was found in Todmorden, 20 miles away, covered in a strange ointment that scientists could not identify.

Weirder still, the policeman who found the body, Alan Godfrey, became involved in a mystery that only Starfleet might be able to explain. While driving in his patrol car near Todmorden five months later, he came across a 'huge rotating, diamond-shaped object hovering five feet off the ground. He lost consciousness for nearly half an hour and woke to find a strange red mark on his foot.' Under hypnosis, he detailed his alien abduction. His story hit the news pages around the world, which saw a stampede of UFOers to West Yorkshire. Since 2008 there have been more than 850 reports of UFO sightings locally. All these stories, the moving lights, the triangular craft glowing green over Holmfirth, are discussed at the regular meetings in the Golden Lion. Only remember to pay the little green man on the door.

**Address** The Golden Lion, Fielden Square, Todmorden, OL14 6LZ, +44 (0)1706 816333, www.goldenliontodmorden.co.uk | **Getting there** The pub is located on the A6033 Rochdale Road on the south bank of the River Calder | **Hours** Thu & Fri 3–10pm, Sat noon–10pm, Sun noon–8pm | **Tip** It's well worth spending a spare day exploring this Victorian-looking market town with its handsome Classical-styled buildings, such as the Town Hall, featuring symbols of both Yorkshire and Lancashire, the Market Hall, and then climbing up to Dobroyd Castle to the south-west of the town, built for mill-owner John Fielden, son of the wonderfully named Honest John Fielden, Social Reformer and MP.

# 93 __ Barbara Hepworth's Family of Man

*It's a family affair*

There is an embarrassment of riches to be found in the Yorkshire Sculpture Park south-west of Wakefield. The park is a sprawling 500-acre open-air expanse of modernist art, a gallery without walls, full of glorious creations. Its collection of Henry Moore works is one of the largest open-air displays of his bronzes in Europe.

Pride of place goes to Barbara Hepworth's *Family of Man*, one of her best-known works. This is a group of nine abstract bronze sculptures, each of which represents a stage of human life, such as *Parent I*, *Parent II* and *Young Girl*. The work dates back to 1970 and has been on display here since 1980, sited away from the trees to give an unobstructed view. Hepworth wanted them to appear as if they had 'risen out of the ground like geological formations'.

Barbara Hepworth was born in Wakefield in 1903, studied at Leeds alongside Henry Moore, and became one of the leading avant-garde figures in the 20th-century international art scene. In Europe, she met such luminaries as Georges Braque and Piet Mondrian. When war broke out in 1939 she moved to St Ives and attracted many followers. She died in tragic circumstances in 1975, in a fire in her home, now preserved as a museum.

Yorkshire Sculpture Park occupies a 500-acre site at Bretton Hall country house. It was Britain's first sculpture park and was based on temporary open air exhibitions that had been organised in London parks by the Arts Council. It also features The Weston, a new £3.6 million gallery built on the site of a former quarry, expertly spliced into the landscape Frank Lloyd Wright style. It is part of the Yorkshire Sculpture Triangle, which also includes The Henry Moore Institute and David Chipperfield's £35 million Hepworth Wakefield art gallery by the River Calder.

**Address** West Bretton, Wakefield, WF4 4LG, +44 (0)1924 832631, www.ysp.org.uk | **Getting there** Just off the A 637 by Junction 38 of the M1 | **Hours** Grounds open daily, except Christmas Eve & Christmas Day; check website for opening hours of indoor galleries and café | **Tip** Stay in the park and head for the Deer Shelter created by James Turrell, the acclaimed 'sculptor of light' as a place of contemplation and revelation. It was commissioned in 2007 by the Art Fund, Britain's leading art charity.

# 94 — Chantry Chapel on Bridge
*Give me that old time religion*

Chantry chapels were mediaeval sites where the clergy would recite special masses to speed up the movement of souls of the dead to heaven – if the family paid enough. They were abolished when Edward VI, England's first Protestant king, took to the throne in 1547. The Protestants deemed them idolatrous, and damned the Catholics for misapplying funds and misappropriating lands. Their assets were stripped and the monies used for financing a new war with France.

Hundreds were demolished, yet Wakefield's – officially the Chantry Chapel of St Mary the Virgin – survived as a warehouse, and later library and cheese shop. It was even painted by Turner. It returned to being a chapel when the Church of England took it over in 1842. The Yorkshire Architectural Society successfully ran the restoration using designs by the leading Gothic revival architect George Gilbert Scott. Unfortunately, he chose Caen stone for the façade, which soon crumbled in the polluted atmosphere.

There are now only four other bridge chantry chapels left in the country. The others are at St Ives in Cambridgeshire, Rotherham, Derby and Bradford-on-Avon. One reason why this survived is because it's a structural part of a bridge – the bridge over the River Calder that dates back to the 1350s. During the Wars of the Roses, the Battle of Wakefield of 1460 took place nearby and resulted in the Earl of Rutland being killed while trying to flee.

Wakefield, the County Town of the old West Riding, a Royalist stronghold during the Civil War, was the Diocese for a huge part of Yorkshire for hundreds of years, until it transferred to Leeds early in the 21st century. Many churches in the area still sport the sign proclaiming Diocese of Wakefield. In 2011, a Wakefield nightclub was caught up in a huge row when it named itself 'Religion', announced club nights called 'Mass', 'Resurrection' and 'Salvation', and sold cocktails with names like 'Angel Wings'.

Address 3 Calder Vale Road, Wakefield, WF1 5DL, +44 (0)1924 373923, www.chantrychapelwakefield.org | Getting there East off the A 61 on the River Calder; train to Wakefield Kirkgate and a five-minute walk | Hours Accessible 24 hours from the outside; check website for details of open days | Tip A mile south are the ruins of Sandal Castle that features briefly in Shakespeare's *Henry VI Part 3*, which is sometimes performed on the site.

# 95 The Messiah's Mansion

*He's not the Messiah, he's a very naughty boy*

Melbourne House is no ordinary mid-19th-century stone mansion. It was built after its creator, John Wroe, was instructed in a dream to create a house where the Messiah could dwell – and John Wroe was that Messiah.

John Wroe was born in Bradford in 1782 and became a farmer. He sired seven children but when he fell ill with the fever in 1819 he began seeing visions and joined a Messianic sect, the Christian Israelites. He soon became their leader, vowing to keep both Mosaic Old Testament law and the gospel of Christ. Adherents dressed modestly and never shaved or cut their hair. Descendants would be immortal as joint rulers with God of an imminent eternal kingdom.

Wroe was publicly baptised in the River Aire at Idle Thorpe witnessed by 30,000 people, some of whom impolitely cried out 'drown him' and taunted him further when his promise to walk on the water failed to materialise. Wroe built his 'new Jerusalem' in Ashton-under-Lyne east of Manchester on the edge of the Peak District. He also announced that he had been commanded from heaven to take 'seven virgins to cherish and comfort [him]'. Remarkably, several local families obliged, but the child that duly appeared was female, which blunted his reputation. Wroe fled to Melbourne, Australia. There he received plentiful donations, which allowed him to return to Yorkshire and build this grand property. The grounds filled several acres, and contained stables and fruit trees. But despite heavenly guidance the house that went up looked rather similar to Melbourne Town Hall. It opened on Whit Sunday 1857 with a ceremony attended by acolytes in white robes administering to 'Prophet' Wroe.

John Wroe died in Australia in 1864, which infuriated those followers who believed in his immortality. For some years his effects remained on show here at Melbourne House in the expectation of a resurrection, yet to be confirmed.

**Address** Brandy Carr Road, Wrenthorpe, Wakefield, WF2 0UG | **Getting there** The mansion on Brandy Carr Road is a mile south of the M1, nearly a mile west of the A650, and a couple of miles north of Wakefield | **Hours** Viewable from the outside only | **Tip** For a more mundane religious experience head to the centre of Wakefield and the impressive cathedral that boasts of the tallest spire in Yorkshire, its appearance mostly the work of the great Victorian Gothicist George Gilbert Scott (London's Albert Memorial and St Pancras Renaissance Hotel.

# 96__British Library, Boston Spa

*'Libraries gave us power'*

It might look like a particular nasty re-education facility beamed in from East Germany at its most communist, and many drive past thinking it's the local prison, but the sign proclaiming British Library should ease concerns. Yes, it's the national library's token northern outpost on an industrial estate near Wetherby, but nevertheless a vital outlet for researchers.

For decades the British Library's aim was to centralise everything: a copy of every British book ever published, every newspaper, pamphlet and document under one roof, but people just kept on producing *stuff*, so new buildings kept being needed. Originally the British Library was housed inside Robert Smirke's 1820s' British Museum building in Bloomsbury. When library bosses announced a plan to demolish a huge estate of streets in front of the Museum, including the property where Sherlock Holmes fictitiously first lived when he came to London, so that a new library could be built opposite, the resistance was phenomenal. Instead, a new library was built in St Pancras in 1997; it took Sandy Wilson 37 years to devise what looks like a giant Tesco, wonderfully denounced by Prince Charles as suiting an academy for the secret police. But at least it was next to three main London railway termini.

A site at Boston Spa started to rise in 1961. In December 2009, a new £26-million building was opened here with a capacity for seven million items. In 2015 it was joined by the National Newspaper Building, which uses robotic cranes to retrieve items in a building that claims to be the most advanced library storage facility in the world, and one of the most air-tight in the country, with some 200 miles of shelf space. Yorkshire collections now make up around 70 per cent of the library's total stock.

**Address** Boston Spa, Wetherby, LS23 7BQ, +44 (0)1937 546000, www.bl.uk | **Getting there** Off the A1(M) five miles east of Wetherby. Follow the signs for Thorp Arch Estate, A1237; train to either York or Leeds stations, followed by a 30-minute taxi ride. | **Hours** Tue–Fri 10.30am–3.30pm; access is free but intending visitors need to apply for a Reader Pass | **Tip** Head north-west to Wetherby itself and then continue for a few miles to the remains of Spofforth Castle where rebel barons might well have drawn up Magna Carta in 1215.

# 97 __ Caedmon's Cross

*Celtic monument to England's first religious poet*

Rising starkly over Whitby 20 feet high is Caedmon's Cross, commemorating the seventh-century Anglo-Saxon poet, and shaped in the Celtic fashion. Caedmon lived in a monastic community, in the days when Whitby was known as Streonaeshalch. He was a religious poet, the earliest named English poet, who learnt to compose songs after a dream. Hilda, the abbess of Whitby, asked him to take the tonsure of a monk. His only surviving work, the Creation hymn, is the oldest recorded poem in English literature.

After having a premonition of his own death, Caedmon was asked to be taken to the monastery hospice, where he died in ad 680. His feast-day is on 11 February. Knowledge of Caedmon comes mostly from the Venerable Bede, the eighth-century Benedictine monk. 'There was in the Monastery of this Abbess a certain brother, particularly remarkable for the Grace of God, who was wont to make religious verses, so that whatever was interpreted to him out of scripture he soon after put the same into poetical expressions of much sweetness and humility.'

The cross is set upon a solid stone-base at the top of the infamous 199 or so steps in the graveyard of St Mary's Church. It looks antiquated but dates back as recently as 1898. It is made from hard sandstone, quarried close by Hadrian's Wall, and is richly decorated. On the east face there are panels featuring Christ blessing, his feet resting upon a dragon and a pig; King David playing a harp; the abbess Hilda with her feet on tiny locally found fossilised creatures (ammonites); and her five favourite scholars. On the west face there is a double vine symbolising Christ and the first nine lines of his hymn of Creation. The other two sides display an English rose, birds, a harp, animals and a tree from the Garden of Eden. In 2012, part of the East Cliff, right near the Cross, fell away leading to calls for Caedmon to be moved.

Address St Mary's Church, Whitby, YO22 4JR, +44 (0)1947 603421, www.whitbymuseum.org.uk | Getting there The churchyard is located on the eastern side of the River Esk at the northern end of the town by the sea | Hours The cross is accessible 24 hours; see website for church hours | Tip Around the cross is the Whitby graveyard, which must rank as the most atmospheric and wildest in England. Some of the gravestones have been literally blown to pieces by the powerful winds and rain lashing in from the North Sea.

# 98 Captain Cook's *Endeavour*

*A seaworthy reminder of Cook's travels*

Anchored in the sea off the coast of Whitby … is it the ship in which Captain Cook sailed the south seas? Not quite; it's a full-scale replica and as a floating museum a new tourist attraction for Yorkshire's leading seaside town.

This *Endeavour* was built in 1993 in Stockton-on-Tees and bought by ex-Naval officer Andrew Fiddler at an auction in 2017. It arrived after a 40-mile trip from Middlesbrough – not quite Tasmania to New Caledonia – to mark the 250th anniversary of Yorkshire-born Cook's first expedition to the Pacific. The arrival of the vessel was greeted by crowds lining the harbour walls and surrounding cliffs as a cannon saluted and bells rang. However, this *Endeavour* was never built to be sailed and was being towed down the coastline.

The original *Endeavour* was built in Whitby in 1764 as the *Earl of Pembroke*. It was meant to be a Whitby Cat (coal and timber ship), hauling the black gold, but the Navy commissioned the vessel and reregistered it as HM *Bark Endeavour*. Captain Cook took command in 1768 for his scientific mission to the Pacific, leaving Plymouth to look for what had been described as *Terra Australis Incognita* – unknown southern land. The crew reached Tahiti in time to observe the 1769 transit of Venus across the Sun, as predicted a century earlier by William Crabtree, a Manchester draper.

After landing at what is now known as Botany Bay in Australia, and nearly running aground on the Great Barrier Reef, which saw Cook throw the guns overboard, *Endeavour* then set sail into the largely uncharted ocean to the south, stopping at various islands, including Tahiti, to claim them for Great Britain. When the ship returned home it was given a more prosaic role taking troops to the Falkland Islands and later in the American War of Independence before being wrecked off the coast of Rhode Island. Relics can be found at various maritime museums.

**Address** Endeavour Wharf, Whitby, YO21 1DN, +44 (0)1947 600511, www.hmbarkendeavour.co.uk | **Getting there** Take the A 171 Middlesbrough–Whitby–Scarborough road. Head for Whitby Harbour – you can't miss the *Endeavour*'s masts silhouetted against the skyline | **Hours** Daily 10am–5pm | **Tip** In the harbour (on Grape Lane YO22 4BA) is the handsome 17th-century house where Captain Cook lodged with the shipowner, John Walker, and which is now a museum with original paintings and drawings from the voyages and models of the ships as well as assorted weirdities from foreign lands.

# 99___Dracula in Whitby

*Bring out your dead*

The invention of Dracula, one of the most infamous characters in English literature – famous throughout the world indeed – has made Whitby a magnet for fans of Gothic horror and those looking for traces of the undead.

Dracula and Whitby are forever connected thanks to Bram Stoker's 1897 novel. The author stayed in a guesthouse at 6 Royal Crescent in 1890, and soon realised the atmospheric seaside town, with its windswept headland, dramatic ruins and a church of swooping bats, was perfect. Even the local precious stone – jet – was associated with mourning. Originally Dracula was going to be called Count Wampyr, but in Whitby Library Stoker found an 1820 book about a William Wilkinson, British consul in Bucharest, which mentioned a 15th-century prince Vlad Tepes, Vlad the Impaler, also known as Dracula – 'son of the dragon' in the local Romanian Wallachian language. Stoker thought Dracula could be a play, *The Undead*, designed so that the great actor Henry Irving could play the lead. But after a test performance Irving said he never wanted to see it again, so Stoker reworked it but retained Irving's characteristics of the histrionic toff for Dracula himself.

In the local taverns, Stoker soaked up salty tales from the salty dogs he met to create the perfect horror tale. A particular favourite was the shipwreck five years back of a Russian vessel, the Dmitri, which ran aground near East Cliff carrying a cargo of silver sand with only the captain left, tied to the wheel. This became the Demeter, the ship that brings Dracula to Whitby with a cargo of silver sand and boxes of earth. In the novel, Dracula's ship runs aground in Whitby and the horrible hero, as a dog, runs up the 199 steps to Whitby Abbey and the graveyard. There he finds his first victim, Swales, a name Stoker found on a headstone. There are goth weekends in Whitby and a variety of Draculatory tours.

**Address** The Dracula Experience, 9 Marine Parade, Whitby, YO21 3PR, +44 (0)1947 601923, www.draculaexperience.co.uk | **Getting there** Take the A171 Middlesbrough–Whitby–Scarborough road. Head for Whitby Harbour, then Haggersgate; train to Whitby station then a 10-minute walk | **Hours** Tours: summer and half-term holidays daily 9.45am–5pm, winter weekends only 9.45am–5pm; Paranormal Nights take place on the first Saturday of each month, 11pm–3am | **Tip** Hours will pass in minutes on a sojourn through the graveyard of St Mary's Church examining the headstones. Many are inscribed with a skull and crossbones, but these aren't for pirates – they simply denote that the deceased was a Freemason.

# 100 Ruins of Whitby Abbey

*Magnificent, majestic, monastic*

The ruins of 13th-century Whitby Abbey, perched high on a cliff, prone to the worst weather in Yorkshire, are one of the most dramatic sights in the county. The location has weathered a long and chequered history although whether Robin Hood really did practise his archery in the tower is not known.

Successive archaeological digs have revealed evidence of a Bronze Age settlement and there may have been a Roman signal station in the third century AD, as the site is half-way between Roman Goldsborough and Ravenscar. The first building on the site was a monastery, founded c. 657, run by Oswy, king of Northumbria, aided by Hilda, abbess of Hartlepool Abbey, and it became one of the most important religious centres in Britain, known as Streoneshalh or Streaneshalch (meaning Fort Bay or Tower Bay).

Whitby as an important religious centre dates from the hosting of a Synod here in the year 664. The meeting resolved the question of whether the church should adopt and follow Celtic (northern) or Roman Christian traditions, in particular over the complicated problem of the shape of the monastic tonsure and more seriously the setting of the date for Easter, something that still defies easy algorithm. Rome won, the leader of the faction claiming his authority came directly from St Peter.

Whitby was sacked by invading Danes in the 860s and the site was derelict for over 200 years. In the 1070s, Reinfrid, a monk, founded a new Benedictine community and a stone church was added in 1100. Further rebuilding took place in the following centuries, and this new Whitby Abbey thrived until the Dissolution of the Monasteries in the 1530s, after which Sir Richard Cholmley bought the buildings. They were abandoned in the 18th century and then ravaged by storm damage in this most exposed spot. More woe came during the Great War when Whitby Abbey was shelled by a German battlecruiser.

**Address** Abbey Lane, Whitby, YO22 4JT, +44 (0)1947 603568, www.english-heritage.org.uk | **Getting there** Whitby is devoid of major roads. Take the A 171 and head to the east town (east of the River Esk) and the northern tip, as close to the sea as feasible. | **Hours** Daily 10am–5pm, booking essential | **Tip** The Whitby Abbey steps are irresistible – 199 lead from ground level, by the sea, up to Whitby Abbey. While climbing and cursing your choice of exercise, watch all the other dupes counting them, because no one can ever agree how many there are. Just don't tell anyone that before the churchyard was closed to burials in the 19th century, mourners had to carry the coffins all the way up.

# 101 Whalebones of Whitby

*'And we did not catch the whale, brave boys …'*

Two 20-foot jaw bones standing proud on the West Cliff of this endlessly enthralling seaside town honour the days when Whitby was the centre of the whaling trade. Ship after ship would brave the ice-cold seas – 'and for Greenland sail away, brave boys' – to hunt the leviathan, the beast of beasts, the monster of monsters, harpooning and chasing them through the water until the whales were exhausted and close to death.

Whaling began in earnest from Whitby in 1753. Over the next 80 years, whalers killed 25,000 seals, 55 polar bears and 2,761 whales. Whaling promised brutal weather, unrivalled excitement and the fear of disaster. All the crew were familiar with Jonah 1, 4: 'Then the Lord sent a great wind on the sea, and such a violent storm arose that the ship threatened to break up.' The few ships that did return successfully would tie a whale's jawbone to the top of the ship's mast as a sign that they had killed the animal. Back on dry land, the blubber was turned into oil used for candles. Whale bones went into corsets, fishing rods and umbrella ribs.

The industry faded away in the 1830s following a number of unsuccessful sorties and the last whaling ship came back to Whitby empty. A whale bone arch was first erected here in 1853, but 100 years later it was taken down (it is now in the local heritage centre) and replaced by jawbones from a 100-ton whale killed by a Norwegian ship. By the end of the 20th century that arch was crumbling away, so it was replaced in 2003 by the bones of a Bowhead whale killed by native Alaskans. The view framed by the huge arch is breathtaking: quaint cottages and cobbled streets overlooked by the ruins of the equally monstrous abbey.

But why was Whitby the whaling port? Why not Scarborough or Saltburn? The answer is simple and brilliant. Whitby is the only location in the entire British Isles that directly faces the North Pole.

**Address** North Terrace, Whitby, YO21 3HA | **Getting there** Head to the north-east tip of the west side of Whitby | **Hours** Accessible 24 hours | **Tip** They don't serve whale, but the queues stretch down the road to dine at the celebrated Magpie fish and chips restaurant. It's not just the quality of the food, which is excellent, but the fact that the waitresses wear 1950s-style mufti.

# 102__Wreck of the
## *Admiral von Tromp*
*'Hoist a hand, or drown amidst this stormy sea'*

It might not be the wreck of the Hesperus, but the *Admiral von Tromp* at Saltwick Bay, just north of Whitby, is as awful a sight.

No one knows how the trawler foundered on 30 October, 1976. The cap'n, Frankie Taal, set off from Scarborough Harbour at 1am, and everything seemed normal as the boat set a course for fishing grounds. The skipper then left the experienced John Addison at the wheel and went for a lie down, safe in the knowledge that when he awoke they would have arrived at their destination.

Instead, he was shaken out of his sleep when the vessel began to heel. One crew member thought the boat had been run down – it surely couldn't have hit the rocks! Taal asked Addison what he was doing, but the latter looked dazed. He sent out a m'aidez and made a brave attempt to save the boat. The crew all put on lifejackets, and he tried to anchor the boat, but – too late. The vessel turned broadside and began to fill with water. Shipmates on dry land even charted the boat's course and discovered it was 90 degrees off course when it sank. It had been heading straight towards some of the worst rocks in the vicinity.

So how could a modern vessel complete with navigational aids run aground on Saltwick Bay? Yes, it was foggy, but that wasn't unusual. According to a senior nautical surveyor, had the boat been left to its own devices it wouldn't have gone off course … it seemed the boat had purposely been driven into the rocks. The one man who could have shed light on the drama, John Addison, drowned. Even the rescue was beset by difficulty. The Whitby Lifeboat tried many times to get near and failed. An investigation found the crew was sober, so it's a mystery that will never be solved. The wreck can be seen at low tide after clambering on the rocks.

**Address** Saltwick Bay, Whitby, YO22 4JX | **Getting there** The only realistic way is by vehicle, taking the road to Saltwick Bay off the A 171 just north of Hawsker. There are minor roads leading south from Whitby. | **Hours** Viewable at low tide | **Tip** Go fossil hunting around the bay itself to discover ammonites, shells, and even jet, the gem that Whitby is most famous for.

# 103— The Unluckiest Pier in the World

*It was long but didn't last long along the seaside*

This pair of crenellated towers, known locally as the Sandcastle, is all that remains of the ill-fated Withernsea Pier on the East Yorkshire coast.

The pier opened in 1878 at the height of the Victorian craze for building long structures out into the sea. It was made of iron girders, stretched out for 1,196 feet, and cost one penny for admission. But happy days in the sun and sea didn't last long. After two years' life, a coal barge collided with it during a storm and wrenched a 200-foot long hole through the middle. In 1890 a fishing boat, the *Genesta*, destroyed more than half the pier. After the *Henry Parr* vessel bound for Grimsby hit it in 1893, only 50 feet remained. The last portion was removed in 1905.

There used to be more than 100 such piers across Britain – from Saltburn to Ryde, from Hove to Llandudno – symbolising a confident empire on which the sun would never set. Brighton's West Pier, now just an iron shell, attracted two million visitors a year. Many sported over-the-top ornate decorations, as money was no object when it came to *fin-de-siècle* grandiosity. Pleasure steamers would dock there; at Southend, the longest, there was even a dinky train to traverse the monstrous length. Piers began to be filled with cafés, bandstands, casinos, swimming pools and concert halls. No seaside holiday in the 1960s was complete without a long walk on a short pier to see some naff light entertainment act such as Peters and Lee or Vince Hill murder some old standards.

In recent decades, the decline of the English seaside town, caused by the fashion to head overseas plus embarrassment at earlier extravaganzas, saw many piers covered over. However, a crowd-funding campaign has been launched to rebuild the one at Withernsea.

**Address** The Promenade, Withernsea, HU19 2JS | **Getting there** Head for the centre of the town on the A1033 east out of Hull; no railway | **Hours** Accessible 24 hours | **Tip** Easily visible is Withernsea's inland lighthouse, which is no longer active and houses a museum with features on locally born 1950s' film star Kay Kendall.

# 104_ York's Terrible Tower
*Apocalypse then*

Anti-Semitic attacks such as Kristallnacht have not just happened only in Germany – even in Yorkshire – and the county was witness to the worst in English history: the massacre at Clifford's Tower, the keep of York Castle, in 1190 when some 150 Jews were killed.

Resentment against York's Jews grew in March 1190 as soldiers prepared to leave on the third Crusade. A mob targeted Jewish homes for looting. The governor of York Castle offered the Jews protection in fortified Clifford's Tower. They accepted, but it backfired. The governor betrayed them.

A mob besieged the keep, a fire broke out, and many of those inside chose to commit suicide rather than be forcibly baptised. Fathers killed their wives and children, and then slayed themselves. Those Jews who didn't kill themselves or die in the fire were murdered by those who saw an opportunity to eradicate their financial debt to the local Jewish population. One of the ringleaders, Richard Malebisse, offered safe passage to any Jews who agreed to convert. The few who took this option were tricked and murdered as soon as they came out from the burning building.

Clifford's Tower was rebuilt in 1250. All Jews in England were expelled on the centenary of the massacre in 1290 and only allowed to return officially in 1656. For centuries it was said there was a Jewish curse on the city, but this was lifted in 1990 at a ceremony conducted by the Chief Rabbi and the Archbishop of York who both unveiled a plaque with a Hebrew inscription from the Book of *Isaiah*.

Few now appreciate the history of Clifford's Tower. At weekends, revellers climb around it. However, once a year a group of Orthodox Jews conducts a remembrance service on the site. Around are planted daffodils whose shape is similar to the Star of David. In 2020, the local Jewish community sought to hire a rabbi for the first time since the Middle Ages.

**Address** Tower Street, York, YO1 9SA, +44 (0)1904 646940, www.english-heritage.org.uk | **Getting there** Follow the A 1036. The tower is a mile east of York train station across the River Ouse. | **Hours** Currently closed for restoration work, but normally open daily summer 10am–6pm, winter 10am–4pm | **Tip** A couple of hundred yards north is the street with one of the most ridiculous names in England: Whip-Ma-Whop-Ma-Gate. It is the shortest street in the city and yet has the longest name. The name was first recorded in 1505 as 'Whitnourwhatnourgate'. A plaque attached to the church here gives the meaning as 'what a street!'

# 105__ The Great North Road

*Historic road to somewhere*

The Great North Road is the greatest road in the history of the island of Great Britain. It was built to link London with Edinburgh and is fittingly numbered the A1, not the A some other number. From the south, the road meets Yorkshire between the obscure villages of Tickhill and Styrrup. Eighty miles later it crosses the old northern boundary of the county, the River Tees, to reach Darlington.

Ancient villages and towns thrived from being on the Great North Road. Places like Wentbridge and Ferrybridge slaked travellers' weary thirst at their great coaching inns. In recent times the traditional route has changed to benefit bigger locations such as Doncaster, Pontefract, Wetherby and Ripon.

The road has caught the imagination of the greatest writers. In *The Pickwick Papers* (1836), Charles Dickens noted how when the mail coaches stopped 'porters were thrusting parcels into every boot, guards were stowing away letter-bags, and hostlers were dashing pails of water against the renovated wheels'. In *The English Mail Coach* (1849), Thomas de Quincey thrilled at how the mail coaches 'distributed over the face of the land … the heart-shaking news of Trafalgar … of Vittoria, of Waterloo'.

So much British history has coincided with this great road, despite its unfortunate connotations with highwaymen such as Dick Turpin. King James journeyed along it all the way from Edinburgh to London in 1603 as James VI of Scotland. When he arrived in London he became James I of England and Scotland. *En route* he would have passed the mail coach, which took nine days to get from London to Edinburgh and vice versa. George IV would travel up the road from London to visit the Doncaster races. Couples would elope on it to get to the Scottish border. It is now used by the odd government special adviser driving from London to Barnard Castle during the Covid lockdowns to test his eyesight.

**Hours** Accessible 24 hours | **Tip** There are hundreds of pubs just off the A 1 in Yorkshire, but try the top of the range Blue Bell at Arkendale, a few miles north-east of Harrogate.

# 106__Alum Pot
*A subterranean potted history*

Alum Pot is one of three spectacular potholes in Simon Fell, the others being Jingle Pot and Hurtle Pot. Alum has a depth of 1,125 feet and at the bottom the water has filled the underground limestone passages of the cave system. Helpfully, a gash in the limestone 300 feet down means that the feature can be entered by rope ladders or by a passage through the limestone known as Long Churn that begins on the moorland.

A stream flows out of Alum Pot, under the river, and emerges in a small circular pool, the Turn Dub, before joining the major Ribble waterway near its source. The shaft is protected by a wall to prevent sheep and people falling down, but the Dales' authorities stress that only those who know what they're doing should go any closer. There is a good view where a stream that falls into Alum Pot crosses the path.

Alum Pot has variously been known as Allan, Alan, Allen, Hellen and Hell'n Pot. Alum itself is aluminium potassium sulphate, a salt used for pickling, and deployed in leather tanning and aftershave. Until the laws tightened against food adulteration in the late 19th century, unscrupulous grocers would lace flour with alum, vast quantities of which being a by-product of the new industries. Alum made the bread whiter and heavier, but also rotted people's stomachs.

In 1847, a John Birbeck undertook the first known, partial, descent of Alum Pot. He returned the following year more successfully. Another successful attempt occurred in 1870 when navvies working on the nearby Settle–Carlisle railway line used a cage and windlass to take people down. In July 1936 tragedy struck: Mabel Binks became the first potholer in the Yorkshire Dales to die when she was hit by a rock while falling down the Main Shaft. It transpired that someone had thrown it down deliberately. Alum Pot has since gone on to claim more lives.

**Address** Selside Farm, Selside, BD24 0HZ | **Getting there** B 4679, eight miles east of Kirkby Lonsdale | **Hours** Accessible 24 hours. These local caves are mostly on private land and the owners charge a small fee – there is a collection box next to the front door of the farm. | **Tip** Near Alum Pot are the similarly ferocious Hurtle Pot and its cousin, Jingle Pot, mostly flooded and only accessible to cave divers. Worryingly, Hurtle Pot is said to be home to frightening boggarts (ancient bogeymen).

# 107 Bedale Leech House

*Suck it and see*

Imagine no vaccines, no antibiotics, no pills. Feeling ill? Here's a nice leech to suck your blood and remove the pox, we hope. It was called bloodletting – leeches would drain impure blood from the body and cure the illness.

Here in Bedale, in the centre of the Yorkshire Dales, is a rare surviving late Georgian Leech House. It is a small, squat, one-storey, brick-built property on the banks of the Bedale Beck. Its purpose was to store live leeches that could be used for medicinal purposes before being sold on to the local apothecary.

Leeches are bloodsucking relatives of earthworms and can be found in bogs and marshes. They were collected mostly by women, transported in small cages, kept in special containers of moist turf and moss, watered with a bracing bevvy from Bedale Beck and warmed by the fireplace. The leech jars were topped with a secure lid and pierced with small air holes. Feeding was not an issue as they could survive for long periods between meals.

Leeches were first used in Egypt about 2,500 years ago. Use of the system peaked in the mid-19th century and the practice died out around 1900. Somehow the Bedale Leech House survived and was put up for sale in 2003 at a knock-down price of £20,000, marketed as a summer house or garden shed.

In case anyone thinks the use of leeches backward and mediaeval, they are still used for healing skin grafts, plastic surgery, fighting blood clots and restoring blood flow to inflamed parts of the body. They are a natural anaesthetic. During operations, micro surgeons, struggling to attach two ends of arteries, often use leeches. As one doctor at the Manchester Burns Unit once explained, 'Leeches are extremely effective. The bite they make with a good anticoagulant is very long lasting'. He could have added that they don't get tired, call in sick or need a mask – just don't tell the patient what's happening.

**Address** Bedale Road, Bedale, DL8 1AN | **Getting there** Just west of the A 1(M); bus 73 or 856 | **Hours** Viewable from the outside, although occasionally open to the public | **Tip** Bedale Hall (DL 8 1AA), a short distance to the west, is a historic manor house with some unusual features, including an ice house and a blind wall (a large pointless piece of brick work to obstruct clear views).

# 108___ Brideshead Revisited
### 'O God, make me good'

It is impossible to see Castle Howard without thinking of its TV role in *Brideshead Revisited*, Evelyn Waugh's majestic war-time novel, the ultimate in lush aesthetic romance. Everything at Castle Howard is larger, bigger, greater. In 1772, Horace Walpole, the writer and art historian, called it a 'town, a fortified city, temples on high places, woods worthy of being each a metropolis of the Druids, vales connected to hills by other woods, the noblest lawn in the world fenced by half the horizon, and a mausoleum that would tempt one to be buried alive'. Even the driveway is through the longest avenue of lime trees in Europe, all 800 of them.

It's not Walpole's writings that bring visitors here but Waugh's, especially after the equally sublime 1981 TV adaptation starring Jeremy Irons, Anthony Andrews and Laurence Olivier, from the days when TV period costume drama meant high culture, rather than Downton Abbey, and Granada could afford to spare no expense taking the cast beyond Castle Howard to locations in Gozo and Venice on the *QE2*.

In war-ravaged England, Captain Charles Ryder finds his troops stationed at Brideshead and the memories of the time he had spent there some 20 years earlier come flooding back. The strong homosexual overtones of the relationship between Charles Ryder (Jeremy Irons) and the blue-eyed blond-locked Sebastian Flyte (Anthony Andrews), fitted in perfectly with changing attitudes in the 1980s, when it was must-see television.

Castle Howard is not actually a castle; the word is often used for a country seat built on the site of a vanished castle. Work on the building started in 1699 and lasted for a century. It is attributed to John Vanbrugh, the society figure and playwright mocked for his status as an architect by the waspish essayist Jonathan Swift who quipped 'Van's genius, without thought or lecture/ Is hugely turn'd to architecture'.

Address Coneysthorpe, North Yorkshire, YO60 7DA, +44 (0)1653 648333, www.castlehoward.co.uk | Getting there Castle Howard is located 20 miles north-east of York, off the A64 | Hours Daily, house 10.30am–1pm, gardens 10am–5pm | Tip The grounds of Castle Howard are filled with treasures, including the Temple of the Four Winds. Originally the Temple of Diana, the goddess of wild animals and the hunt, it is partly modelled on Andrea Palladio's 16th-century Villa Rotonda in Vicenza and was used by the family as a place of refreshment and reading.

# 109__Druids' Temple, Masham

*Yorkshire's Stonehenge, 200, not 2,000, years old*

Has Stonehenge been moved to Yorkshire? No, this is William Danby's druids' temple, more accessible than its Wiltshire cousin, created in 1803 in a distinctly Spinal Tap form of Stonehenge and set in a small wooded area in Fearby, two miles from Masham.

Danby, a one-time Sheriff of Yorkshire, was an eccentric landowner, and his stony henge was an unusual and ingenious remedy to local unemployment figures. He paid his workers a shilling a day to set up the menhirs, dolmens and sarsens. Once the project was finished, Danby set a challenge. He offered a salary to anyone brave or mad enough to live on the site as a hermit for seven years. He found an anonymous dupe in the 1820s, willing to spend the time speaking to no one, Meher Baba style, while allowing his beard and hair to grow uncut. He lasted four years.

Interest in ancient Druidism surfaced in the 19th century when society began to learn that druids weren't simply pagan mystics, but that they were teachers, judges, political leaders and philosophers comparable to the Magi and the Brahmans of India, as well as mediators between man and God. Unfortunately, most texts about them were written by non-druids, particularly Julius Caesar, and to add to the confusion, their doctrine prevented them from recording their knowledge in writing as they dealt solely by word of mouth. But as *History Today* wrote in 2009: 'Archaeology has proved unenlightening. Not a single artefact has been turned up which experts universally agree to be Druidic.'

Unsurprisingly, over the years this site has been used for devil worship, mystic practices and bizarre rituals, as Baroness Masham of Ilton cited in a speech to the House of Lords in 2000. Nowadays it attracts New Age pilgrims around the time of the summer solstice and winter equinox. One can even imagine being accosted by a disciple from *Brookside*'s Stones of Shad sect.

**Address** Knowle Lane, Fearby, HG4 4JZ, +44 (0)1765 535020 | **Getting there** The temple is 10 miles west of the A 1(M) and 10 miles north-west of Ripon | **Hours** Accessible 24 hours | **Tip** Peculiar to Masham is the Peculiar of Masham, a harlequin-like figure based on local crusader Roger de Mowbray and known far and wide as the logo on bottles of Theakston's ales. In olden times, civic and religious affairs were presided over by the Peculiar of Masham – am ecclesiastical court of 24 men that still exists and rules on matters such as drunkenness and brawling.

# 110_ Forbidden Corner Follies
*Fruits of the forbidden follies*

It's totally bonkers and beyond belief, but it's real, realer than real, surreal! The Forbidden Corner, by its own admission, is 'the strangest place in the world', a labyrinth of tunnels, chambers, surprises and follies within a four-acre garden in Tupgill Park amid the Yorkshire Dales.

Its features include the Temple of the Underworld, the Eye of the Needle, a pyramid of translucent glass, paths and passages that lead nowhere, a maze, and water sprays that catch you if you stop. Indeed, the site is filled with tricks and treats at every turn. The Mausoleum scares the kids rotten, while the Cat and Mouse experience, a network of underground tunnels with life-sized sculptures, will bring back the laughter.

The Forbidden Corner was the brainchild of Colin Armstrong and Malcolm Tempest. But it began as something completely different in 1979: a small wood of fir trees created as a wind break to the stables. Ten years later they planted a small bower to enjoy the view down the Coverdale valley. A high wall would shelter the area from high winds and a walled garden followed. Gradually the idea of a grotto grew into a 25-foot-deep hole. When that flooded after heavy rains, a channel had to be dug to take the water away. Digging uncovered underground springs, but what the hell? Another feature in the making! To extend and expand the grotto, ideas were taken from around the country. Portmeirion, the impossibly lovely Welsh model village used in *The Prisoner* TV programme, was a particular inspiration.

In 1994, the private folly opened to the public. Entrance is through the Face Tower which burps as one walks in. Within four years, Forbidden Corner was attracting more than 80,000 visitors. Everyone was happy, apart from the Yorkshire Dales planning officers who nearly got the place closed down. After a huge public campaign the infamous folly was saved.

**Address** Tupgill Park Estate, Coverham, Leyburn, DL8 4TJ, +44 (0)1969 640638, www.theforbiddencorner.co.uk | **Getting there** Take the A 6108 to Middleham followed by Coverham Lane; train to Northallerton or Darlington then bus to Leyburn | **Hours** Daily 1 Apr–31 Oct, then Sun until Christmas, Mon–Sat noon–6pm, Sun 10am–6pm (or dusk, if earlier) | **Tip** You'll need a breather after all that madness, so take a strenuous walk along the Leyburn Shawl, a limestone scar that stretches almost two miles west.

# 111 Ribblehead Viaduct

*Vainglorious Victoriana via the valley*

England's most glorious railway viaduct carries the Settle-Carlisle line over an undulating moor near the Yorkshire-Cumbria border. The viaduct is a remarkable example of Victorian engineering on what was the last railway in Britain to be built entirely with manual labour. The line can claim to be the most remote and isolated in England with the steepest of gradients encompassing 20 viaducts and 14 tunnels. Nevertheless, the viaduct is only a short walk from Ribblehead station.

In 1868, a Tasmanian called Sharland walked the entire 72 miles. On bleak Blea Moor he was caught in a blizzard that saw him holed up in a lonely inn for weeks. Work began in 1869 using more than 2,000 navvies who lived with their families in nearby shanty towns. The remains of some of the camps, with wonderful names – Batty Wife Hole, Sebastopol and Belgravia – can still be seen. But the line's romantic status belies its tragic creation. Hundreds lost their lives. There are unmarked graves of 25 of its builders in Dentdale's St John the Evangelist churchyard, Cowgill. Around 80 people died at Batty Green alone after a smallpox epidemic.

The line finally opened in 1876. Passengers now trying to travel between the two towns on a variety of out-of-the-way lines, that had previously been subjected to Brobdingnagian rules, no longer had to worry about being turfed off trains when a new station meant a different operating company. Due to its remoteness, the line suffers from annual outbreaks of weather. In 1946, it was blocked by snow for two months. Worse still, in the 1970s, it was regularly threatened with closure. But regular protest campaigns introduced the line to a new generation and the government backed down in 1989. The best trips are those on special steam trains. Many embark at Dent Station to explore the dales on foot and visit the village, four miles away.

**Address** Low Sleights Road, near Ingleton, LA6 3AU | **Getting there** Best by train as the viaduct is a short walk from Ribbleshead station. By car, take the Low Sleights Road, the B 6255, off the A 65 at Ingleton. | **Hours** Accessible 24 hours | **Tip** Make a weekend of it and stay nearby at the Old Hill Inn, originally a farm that dates back to 1615. Perfect for accommodation, food, beer and a base for walking.

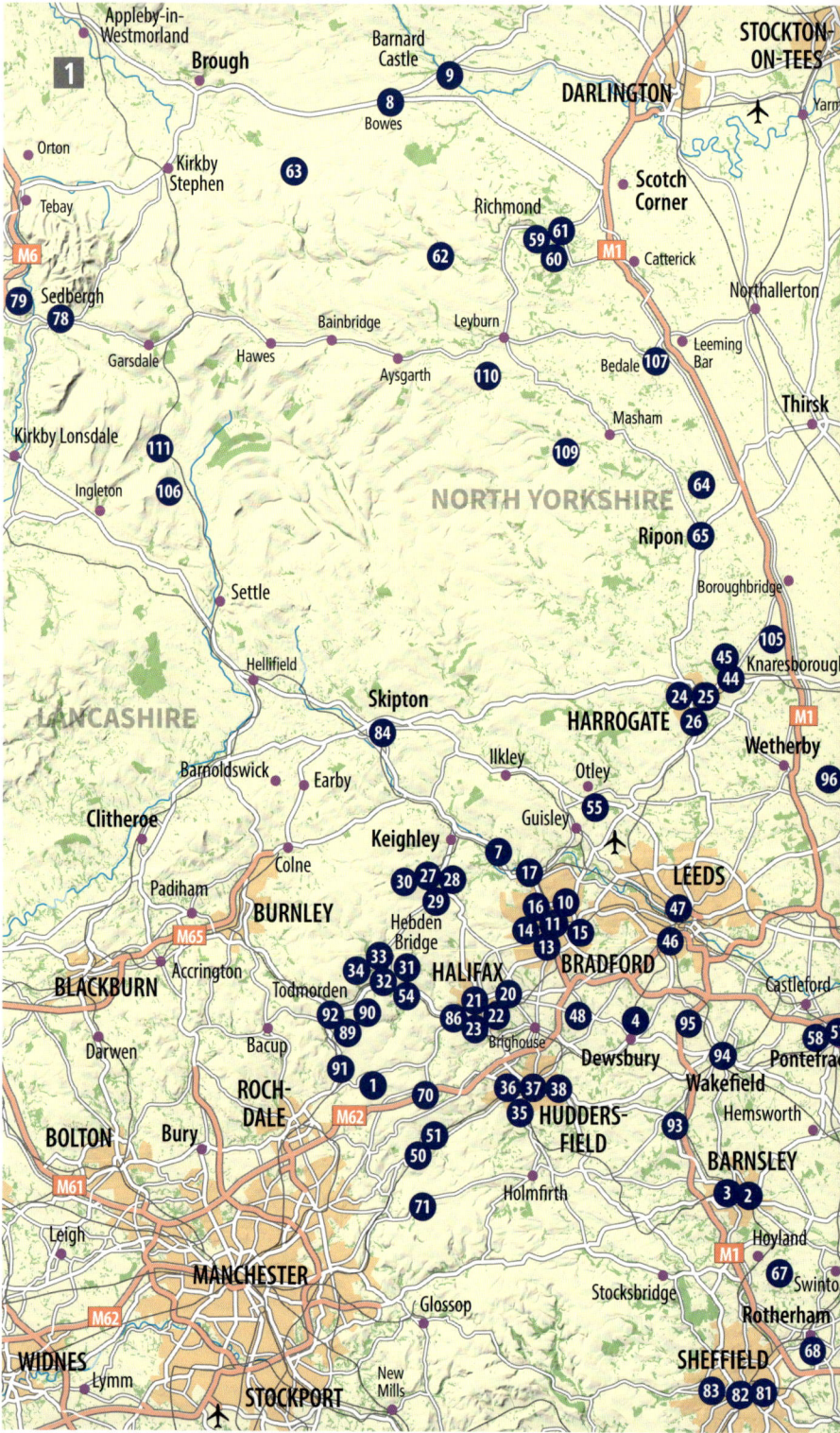

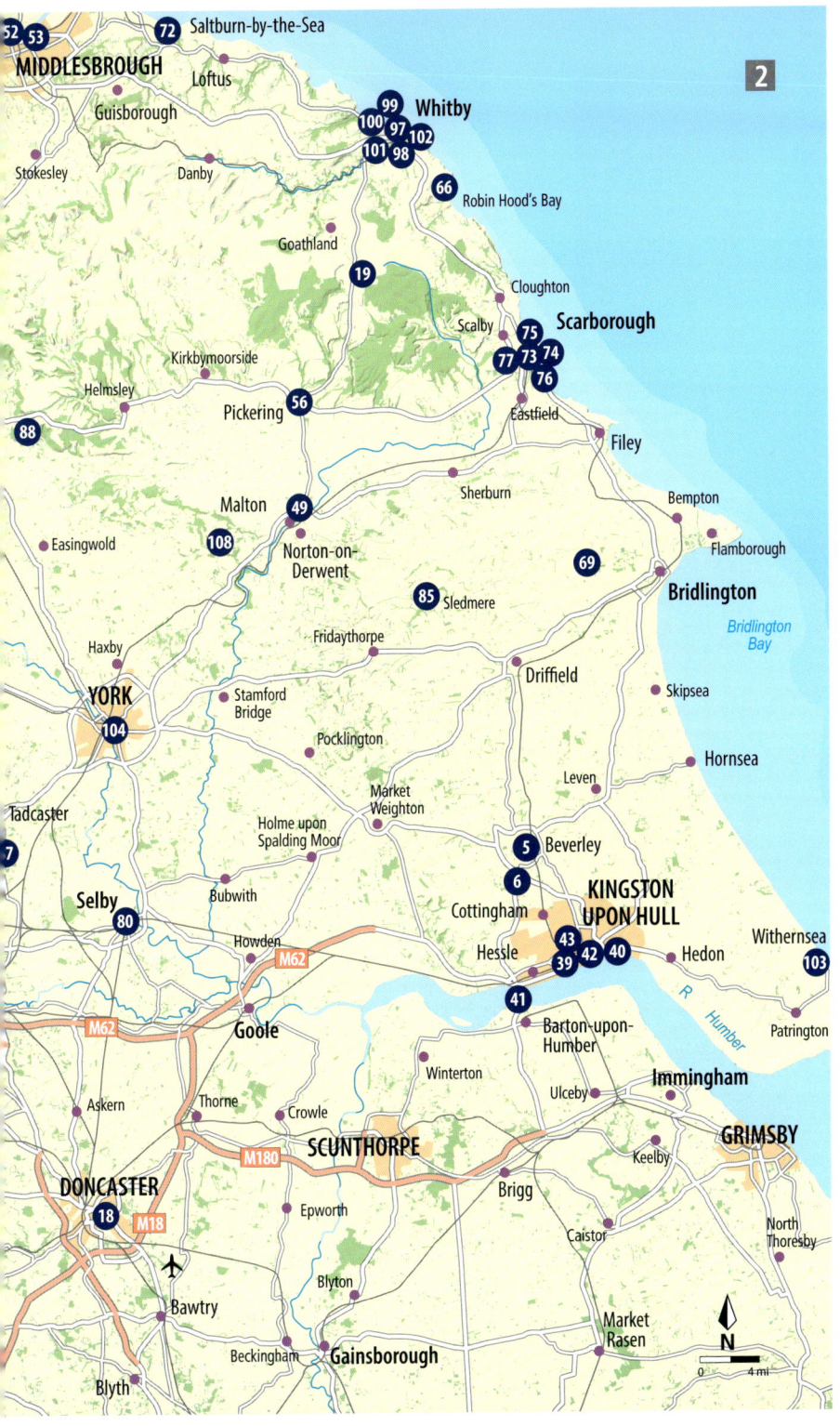

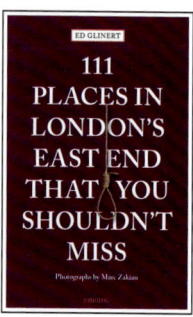

Ed Glinert, Marc Zakian
**111 Places in London's East End That You Shouldn't Miss**
ISBN 978-3-7408-0752-8

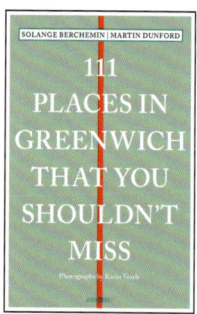

Solange Berchemin, Martin Dunford, Karin Tearle
**111 Places in Greenwich That You Shouldn't Miss**
ISBN 978-3-7408-1107-5

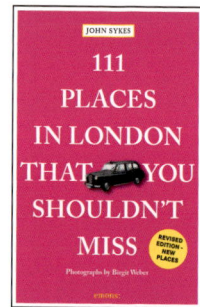

John Sykes, Birgit Weber
**111 Places in London That You Shouldn't Miss**
ISBN 978-3-7408-1168-6

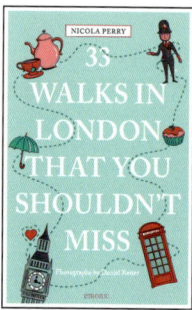

Nicola Perry, Daniel Reiter
**33 Walks in London That You Shouldn't Miss**
ISBN 978-3-95451-886-9

Kirstin von Glasow
**111 Gardens in London That You Shouldn't Miss**
ISBN 978-3-7408-0143-4

Laura Richards, Jamie Newson
**111 London Pubs and Bars That You Shouldn't Miss**
ISBN 978-3-7408-0893-8

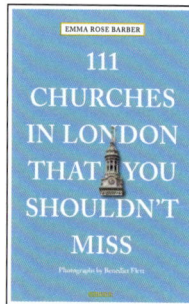

Emma Rose Barber, Benedict Flett
**111 Churches in London That You Shouldn't Miss**
ISBN 978-3-7408-0901-0

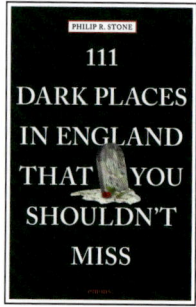

Philip R. Stone
**111 Dark Places in England That You Shouldn't Miss**
ISBN 978-3-7408-0900-3

Solange Berchemin
**111 Places in the Lake District That You Shouldn't Miss**
ISBN 978-3-7408-0378-0

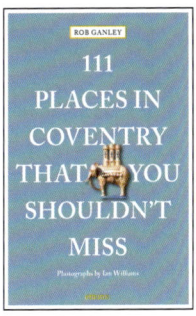

Rob Ganley, Ian Williams
**111 Places in Coventry**
**That You Shouldn't Miss**
ISBN 978-3-7408-1044-3

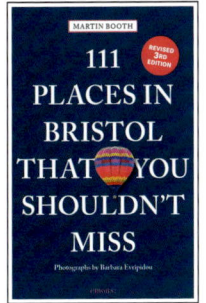

Martin Booth, Barbara Evripidou
**111 Places in Bristol**
**That You Shouldn't Miss**
ISBN 978-3-7408-0898-3

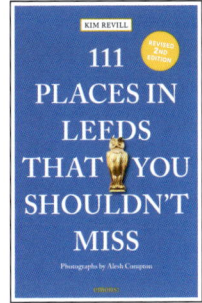

Kim Revill, Alesh Compton
**111 Places in Leeds**
**That You Shouldn't Miss**
ISBN 978-3-7408-0754-2

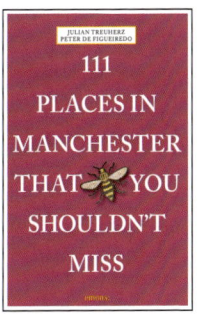

Julian Treuherz,
Peter de Figueiredo
**111 Places in Manchester**
**That You Shouldn't Miss**
ISBN 978-3-7408-0753-5

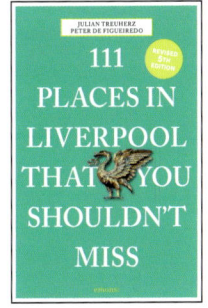

Julian Treuherz,
Peter de Figueiredo
**111 Places in Liverpool**
**That You Shouldn't Miss**
ISBN 978-3-95451-769-5

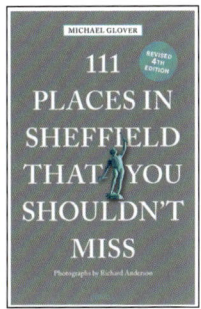

Michael Glover,
Richard Anderson
**111 Places in Sheffield**
**That You Shouldn't Miss**
ISBN 978-3-7408-0022-2

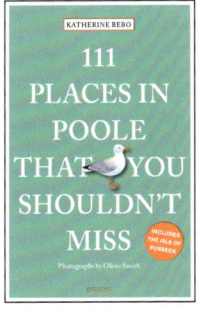

Katherine Bebo, Oliver Smith
**111 Places in Poole**
**That You Shouldn't Miss**
ISBN 978-3-7408-0598-2

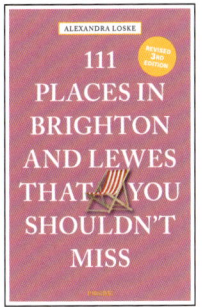

Alexandra Loske
**111 Places in Brighton**
**and Lewes That You**
**Shouldn't Miss**
ISBN 978-3-7408-0255-4

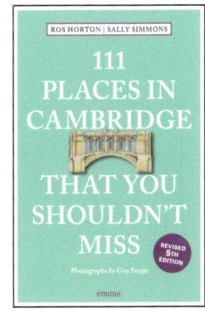

Rosalind Horton,
Sally Simmons, Guy Snape
**111 Places in Cambridge**
**That You Shouldn't Miss**
ISBN 978-3-7408-0147-2

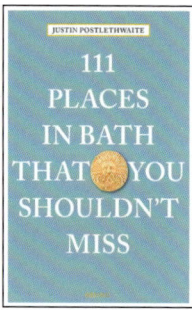

Justin Postlethwaite
**111 Places in Bath That
You Shouldn't Miss**
ISBN 978-3-7408-0146-5

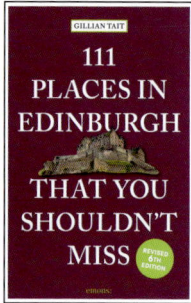

Gillian Tait
**111 Places in Edinburgh
That You Shouldn't Miss**
ISBN 978-3-95451-883-8

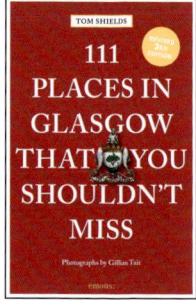

Tom Shields, Gillian Tait
**111 Places in Glasgow
That You Shouldn't Miss**
ISBN 978-3-7408-0256-1

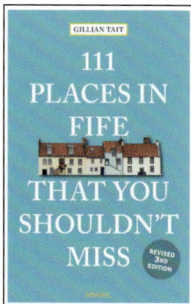

Gillian Tait
**111 Places in Fife That
You Shouldn't Miss**
ISBN 978-3-7408-0597-5

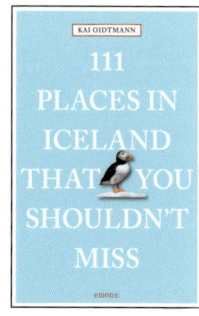

Kai Oidtmann
**111 Places in Iceland
That You Shouldn't Miss**
ISBN 978-3-7408-0030-7

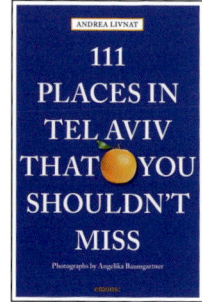

Andrea Livnat,
Angelika Baumgartner
**111 Places in Tel Aviv
That You Shouldn't Miss**
ISBN 978-3-7408-0263-9

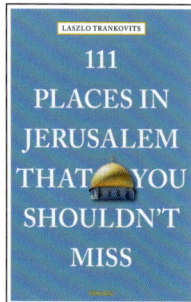

Laszlo Trankovits
**111 Places in Jerusalem
That You Shouldn't Miss**
ISBN 978-3-7408-0320-9

Sybil Canac, Renée Grimaud,
Katia Thomas
**111 Places in Paris
That You Shouldn't Miss**
ISBN 978-3-7408-0159-5

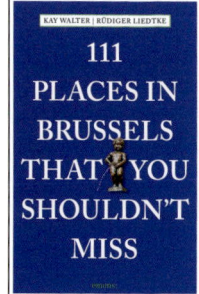

Kay Walter, Rüdiger Liedtke
**111 Places in Brussels
That You Shouldn't Miss**
ISBN 978-3-7408-0259-2

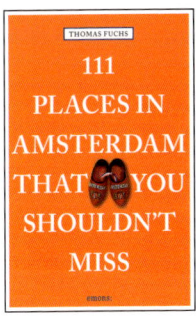

Thomas Fuchs
**111 Places in Amsterdam
That You Shouldn't Miss**
ISBN 978-3-7408-0023-9

Jan Gralle, Vibe Skytte,
Kurt Rodahl Hoppe
**111 Places in Copenhagen
That You Shouldn't Miss**
ISBN 978-3-7408-0580-7

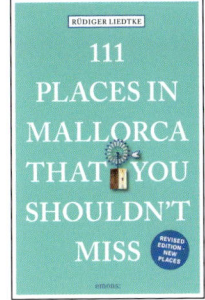

Rüdiger Liedtke
**111 Places in Mallorca
That You Shouldn't Miss**
ISBN 978-3-7408-1049-8

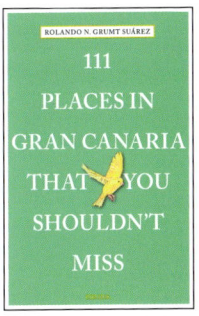

Rolando N. Grumt Suárez
**111 Places in Gran Canaria
That You Shouldn't Miss**
ISBN 978-3-7408-0604-0

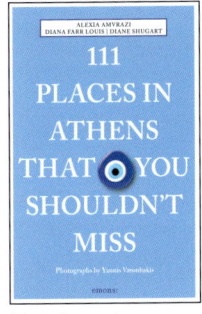

Alexia Amvrazi,
Diana Farr Louis, Diane Shugart,
Yannis Varouhakis
**111 Places in Athens
That You Shouldn't Miss**
ISBN 978-3-7408-0377-3

Catrin George Ponciano
**111 Places along the Algarve
That You Shouldn't Miss**
ISBN 978-3-7408-0381-0

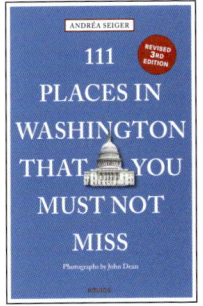

Andréa Seiger, John Dean
**111 Places in Washington
That You Must Not Miss**
ISBN 978-3-7408-0258-5

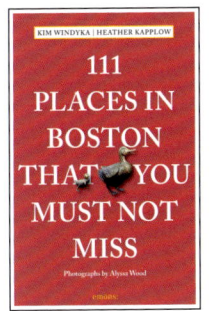

Kim Windyka,
Heather Kapplow, Alyssa Wood
**111 Places in Boston
That You Must Not Miss**
ISBN 978-3-7408-0894-5

Jo-Anne Elikann
**111 Places in New York
That You Must Not Miss**
ISBN 978-3-95451-052-8

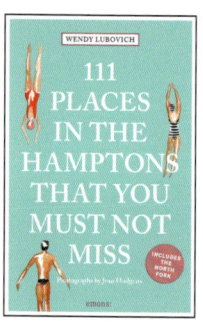

Wendy Lubovich, Jean Hodgens
**111 Places in the Hamptons
That You Must Not Miss**
ISBN 978-3-7408-0751-1

Amy Bizzarri, Susie Inverso
**111 Places in Chicago
That You Must Not Miss**
ISBN 978-3-7408-1030-6

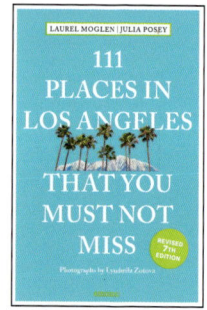

Laurel Moglen, Julia Posey,
Lyudmila Zotova
**111 Places in Los Angeles
That You Must Not Miss**
ISBN 978-3-7408-0906-5

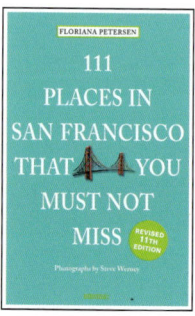

Floriana Petersen,
Steve Werney
**111 Places in San Francisco
That You Must Not Miss**
ISBN 978-3-95451-609-4

Floriana Petersen,
Steve Werney
**111 Places in Silicon Valley
That You Must Not Miss**
ISBN 978-3-7408-0493-0

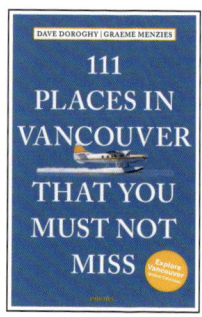

Dave Doroghy,
Graeme Menzies
**111 Places in Vancouver
That You Must Not Miss**
ISBN 978-3-7408-0494-7

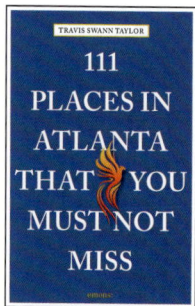

Travis Swann Taylor
**111 Places in Atlanta
That You Must Not Miss**
ISBN 978-3-7408-0747-4

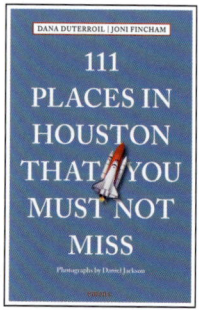

Dana DuTerroil,
Joni Fincham, Daniel Jackson
**111 Places in Houston
That You Must Not Miss**
ISBN 978-3-7408-0896-9

Kelsey Roslin, Nick Yeager,
Jesse Pitzler
**111 Places in Austin
That You Must Not Miss**
ISBN 978-3-7408-0748-1

Many thanks to Alistair Layzell for his unflinching help and patience. A massive thank you to photographer David Taylor, editor Ros Horton and Laura Olk at Emons head office. Then there are the indispensable friends and relatives: John Breslin, Mike Conniff, Katy Walsh Glinert, Emma Marigliano, Patti-Pea, Juliet Rose, Simon Rose, David Stone, Lindsay Sutton, and my quiz teams at the Fox & Goose and Stubbing Wharf, Hebden Bridge.
*Ed Glinert*

For their invaluable help and patience, I'd like to thank Chris Southwell at Calderdale Museum Services, Helga Pearson at the Georgian Theatre Royal, Sharon at the Cabinet of Curiosities, John Reeves at the Forbidden Corner, Sophie Allanby at Castle Howard, the Reverend Gareth Atha at St Peter and St Paul's in Pickering, Kerrie Woolas at Ye Olde White Harte, Rosalind Turner, Sir James and Lady Graham at Norton Conyers, Darren and Nicci at the Wuthering Heights Inn, Jay Stelling at Mother Shipton's Cave, Ruth Burke-Kennedy at Bettys, Christopher Mason and the staff at Harrogate Turkish Baths, Becky and Louisa at Arvon, Alison White at the Bowes Museum, Jennifer Cooke at Selby Abbey, Kay Stevenson at KCOM, and Jasper Hegar and Hana Mitcheson at Leeds University. I'd also like to thank my wife, Tania, who put up with me disappearing for days on end into deepest Yorkshire and who was always there with a smile on my return.
*David Taylor*

## Sources
Ch. 32 *Heptonstall* from *Ted Hughes Collected Poems*, ed. Paul Keegan, Faber & Faber, 2012.
Ch. 34 *Remains of Elmet* from *Ted Hughes Collected Poems*, ed. Paul Keegan, Faber & Faber, 2012.
Ch. 54 Hughes, Ted, *The Iron Man*, Faber & Faber, 2005.
Ch. 43 *Annus Mirabilis* from *Philip Larkin Collected Poems*, ed. Anthony Thwaite, Faber & Faber, 2014.

**Ed Glinert** was born in Dalston, London. He studied Maths and Classical Hebrew at Manchester University, but not at the same time. He worked for *Private Eye* magazine for more than 10 years, and has written a number of books for major publishers including *The London Compendium* and *East End Chronicles* for Penguin. He is one of Britain's most prolific tour guides, working in London, Manchester, Liverpool and West Yorkshire, and gives talks on cruise ships and for the Arts Society.

Newcastle-born **David Taylor** is a professional freelance landscape photographer and writer who now lives in Northumberland. His first camera was a Kodak Instamatic. Since then he's used every type of camera imaginable: from bulky 4x5 film cameras to pocket-sized digital compacts. David has written nearly 40 books about photography, as well as supplying images and articles to both regional and national magazines. His first book for Emons was *111 Places in Newcastle That You Shouldn't Miss*. When David is isn't outdoors he can be found at home with his wife, a cat, and a worryingly large number of tripods.